in memory

of

Adèle de Leeuw

Joanne E. Merkler
6/11/14

REMEMBERED WITH LOVE:

Letters to my Sister

Remembered with Love:

Letters to my Sister

Biographical Sketches by

Adèle De Leeuw

THE BROOKDALE PRESS

Stamford, Connecticut

Library of Congress Cataloging in Publication Data

DeLeeuw, Adèle, 1899-
  Remembered with love.

  Letters addressed to Cateau De Leeuw.
  Summary: After the death of her artist sister, the
author reminisces about their shared childhood, pets,
career experiences, and years of collaboration on books
for children.
      1. DeLeeuw, Adèle, 1899-   —Biography.
  2. De Leeuw, Cateau—Biography. 3. Authors, American—
  20th century-Biography. 4. Artists—United States—
  Biography. 5. Children's literature—Authorship.
  [1. DeLeeuw, Adèle. 2. De Leeuw, Cateau. 3. Authors,
  American. 4. Artists. 5. Authorship. 6. Brothers and
  sisters] I. De Leeuw, Cateau. II. Title.
  PS3507.E463Z47   818'.5209 [B] [920]   81-86639
  ISBN 0-912650-03-6   AACR2

For information, address the publisher:
THE BROOKDALE PRESS
184 Brookdale Road,
Stamford, Connecticut 06903

ISBN: 0-912650-03-6

Library of Congress Catalog Card Number: 81-86639

Manufactured in The United States of America by
RAY FREIMAN & COMPANY

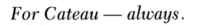

For Cateau — always.

REMEMBERED WITH LOVE:

Letters to my Sister

June

My dearest,

You've gone. And I can never get you back again—except by talking to you. It's childish, I know. But perhaps it will give me some relief from the pent-up sorrow that makes me feel as if my heart will burst.

How often we gently scorned the people who used euphemisms for death! "She has left us." "He has passed over." Where was their strength, we wondered, that they could not acknowledge death for what it was, and speak of it as death? I understand them a little better now. But at least I will demand of myself the will to call death by its own name.

I know what they were trying to do. They were attempting to conceal the ultimate finality . . . at least until they

4

could bear it. Nature bestows a numbness on us at first, giving us time to adjust to the brutal truth. But the numbness does not last long enough, and the truth breaks through the veil and stabs us again and again.

Friends have been marvelous. They have surrounded me with affection and concern; they talk or fall silent as they perceive my mood; they bring gifts of flowers or themselves; they plan little outings and include me in their gatherings. They write letters that make the tears stream down my face, because they appreciated you so . . . they tell me, in warm words, how sweet you were, how brilliant, how witty, how talented, and how blessed they were to know you. It is a comfort to read of their appreciation, to realize that they were aware of all your wonderful qualities. But my loss, as I go over their words, grows greater and greater. I am utterly bereft. I have been abandoned; I feel as if a part of me has been amputated. For we were so close, we knew each other so well, we were so attuned to each other's moods—different though we were in a dozen respects.

There was one letter that helped me more than most. It came from an editor whom you never met. She told me something which has been a kind of bulwark, for she said, "No one truly dies who is remembered with love."

And I know this is true. I remember you with

love, I remember everything about you with undying love. When I think I cannot stand the loneliness any more, something will come to mind, something that I loved in you and it gives me the courage, if only momentarily, to go on.

So that is what I will do, as I write to you. I will think of the things that made our life together the charmed experience it was. I will remember you with love.

July

Toto, dear,

The sun is hot in the garden, but here on the porch it is cool and shady, with dapplings of light flickering through the screen. Tom-Tom rouses himself every once in a while from his spot on the flagstones and chases a shaft of light which he pretends is a butterfly, though I am sure he knows better. But because I am busy writing and have no time for him he is inventing a game of his own and eventually hopes to get me to join him.

Tom-Tom was never your dog, as Tippy was. Tippy was totally yours. I can see you holding him close on your shoulder, his black muzzle near your ear, your white hand on his thick gray coat, and you would say, "Sometimes I think I love him too much."

But of course you didn't mean that. You only

meant that you had a premonition of what it would mean when you lost him. And when he died you were utterly bereft.

I could say that, too—"Sometimes I think I love you too much." And I would not mean it, either. For I cannot love you too much. Having you was the richest treasure of my life, and now I must live on the stored wealth.

The sound of water trickling over the rocks and down into the pool in the garden is a kind of music to accompany my thoughts. What a big decision it was for us to have it! When we bought this house and had the landscape artist plan the garden, his suggestion of a pool met with instant approval. But when he said we could have a recirculating pump and a trickle pouring over the rocks we hesitated. More expense . . . things were piling up on us anyhow. I looked at you and you looked at me, and almost simultaneously we said, "Why not? It will be lovely on hot summer days."

How adventuresome and reckless one feels when one says mentally, "Hang the expense!" It did us both good. We could do without more sheets or pots and pans or that occasional chair we had planned on. Eventually we could have those, too—we hoped. Meanwhile there would be music and coolness in the garden.

8

And eventually we had a frog who decided to live there, and guppies and goldfish. Of course the neighbor's cat got the goldfish and the guppies, but the frog stayed on, hopping out on the rocks at intervals and crossing the grass where Tippy would find him. The frog would freeze while Tippy barked madly and made futile passes at it. It was amusing to watch the little game, and when Frog made a swift leap back to safety we applauded.

It was fun to plant the garden around the pool . . . narcissus and daffodils in the background, scilla and grape hyacinths and tulips and Grecian windflowers and aconite in front. To set the bulbs in the hard November ground and watch for the first yellow glint of aconite in the spring, with snow still on the rocks. The garden has grown and prospered—and changed—over the years, but there has never been quite the thrill of that first spring in our new home with our new garden.

I suppose that has always been the case. The first accomplishment, the first flower, the first of anything you have lived and worked for is the supreme moment, which nothing afterward can quite match. The first check I got for a poem sent me shrieking through the house, and Father said, with his wonderful smile, "Make the most of it, my dear. When you get a thousand dollar check it won't be half the moment this is." And when you sold your first painting you went around on a private cloud for days on end. Nothing after that really matched *that* supreme moment.

We were fortunate in the parents we had. They gave us creative toys and played with us and encouraged our first tentative efforts to express ourselves. They taught us to read at three—how educators scoff at that now!—and to invent plays and to make music and to look through a magnifying glass at the wonders of a blade of grass or a split apple seed or a dandelion. They helped us grow and nurtured our creativity and rejoiced in our successes, as they came along, and helped us rise above our failures. These are things for which we were always grateful, and now more than ever I appreciate the strength their loving concern built into us.

I will need all the strength they gave me and all the strength I have slowly acquired to meet the years ahead. I turn my thoughts away from that, for underneath I am not ready to meet the truth which I know is waiting for me to acknowledge.

It seems ridiculous to think that once I resented you . . . you who have meant everything to me. Of course, it was logical in a way. I had been the only child for four years, adored, petted, made much of. I had my parents' entire attention. And then, one summer evening, they asked how I would like a baby sister or brother. I said quite promptly that I wouldn't. After a while I asked which it would be, and was told there was no choice. It took me days of wrestling with myself—and melting under Mother's gentle charm—to say that if I had to have one or the other I'd probably take a sister. Fortunately for me—and for Mother and Father!—it turned out to be a sister.

I recall, as if it were yesterday, how I stared at you in utter disbelief when I saw you that first morning. Prudence, the maid, had spent the night with me in my bedroom. I heard nothing all night—and in the morning was ushered into Mother's bedroom to see you bundled up in a blanket on a chair. You looked like the kind of doll I wished for . . . . dark hair, a round face, and the most astonishing purple-blue eyes. They looked at me solemnly, and I looked back. This wasn't so bad, I thought reluctantly, but time would tell.

I thought you *were* a doll for a while. When you were placed on the floor on a blanket I squatted down and gave you a push, and you toppled over just like those rubber figures that were popular then. I waited for you to bounce back, as they did, but you didn't. Instead you cried and Mother came running. My explanation didn't go down too well, but she did understand, and you weren't really harmed. Later I tried pushing you off the lower steps of the stairs, and you didn't bounce back then, either. It was disappointing, and I really took little interest in you until you were able to play with me.

That was when I began to realize what a treasure I had. A playmate right in the house! There were so few children anywhere near my age in the neighborhood. Someone I could order around, someone to cuddle when I felt like it, someone I could feel superior to. It was quite a heady feeling.

It's interesting, looking back, to realize how subtly things changed. I didn't order you around too much—you didn't take it. I only felt superior to you on occasions, mostly where learning was concerned. And you became the ideal companion, although at times I resented the fact that I was responsible for you. Then, one day, you became my champion, and things really changed.

The long curls I had were boys' delight. They yanked them in school or whenever they could catch up with me. I had to call for you at kindergarten, after I was out at lunchtime, and a boy down the street came up and pulled one of my curls so hard that I burst out crying. You, tiny as you were, went up to him and made a fist. You looked up and said, in a voice I had never heard before, "You leave my sister alone or I'll punch you in the nose!" It didn't even strike me funny that he was three times as big as you were and could have disposed of you with one swipe of his hand. Instead he looked cowed and turned away, and we went home, you swelling with pride that you had vanquished an enemy, and I nearly bursting with the knowledge that I had such a defender.

We never seemed to lack for something to do, and later on we learned, to our amazement, that our 'attention span' was outstanding. There were soap bubbles to blow, and birds' funerals to conduct, with appropriate music, sung by ourselves, and burial under the honeysuckle hedge; there were plays to invent and put on. . . . you always insisted on being the villain, which was fine with me, because I preferred to be the princess, who was generally rescued by the prince, a delightful boy who lived on the street beyond our back garden. You loved to be killed and fall down in a very realistic fashion with a loud thump, or better yet, to stab someone—in the name of justice, of course—with your rubber dagger and then pull it out and pretend there was blood dripping from it. Black Hand was you favorite character, and in the interests of authenticity, you usually had at least one black hand.

And of course there were stories to tell one another. We read omnivorously, anything and everything we could lay our hands on, and nothing in our parents' library was forbidden us. It was much more pleasant to make up a story ourselves. I don't recall just how we got into it, but we developed a turn-about affair between us that was eminently satisfactory. Maybe I started it, maybe you did—your inventiveness was startling, even at an early age—but anyhow, one of us began a story and the other had to be the attentive listener. We used the cliff-hanger technique and at the end of the tale there was the question hanging in the air. Then what happened? We didn't know it then, but that was our training for the professional story-telling that engaged both of us later on. Next day, if I had begun the tale, you took over and carried it and the people forward into a new adventure, and I was the listener. The following day I had to go on from there.

We never missed a day, or, if we did, we had two installments to cover in one session. As the years went by the story grew more complex and more sophisticated so that, eventually, it bore scant resemblance to the kind of story we had started out with. It went on for years and, as we used to say in our lectures, perhaps we were the originators of the soap opera.

The storytelling time was particularly good for rainy or snowy days. Then we could sit in front of the hearth with the cozy hissing of the seasoned logs burning in the grate, with a dish of popcorn in front of us, or marshmallows to toast over the flames on long forks. It always astonished—and annoyed—us to find that our companions, when we played other games, were so soon satisfied with whatever we were doing. We would just be into a game of hide-and-seek and it was getting exciting, we thought, when someone would say petulantly, "I'm tired of this. Let's play marbles." Reluctantly we would go along with the suggestion, for we never won out on having the first game continue, and would be nicely into marbles when someone else would rise and shout, "Who wants to play Indian?" And everyone—except ourselves—would vote for it. This went on and on, and invariably we were defeated, and try as we would, we could never understand it. The short attention span of most of our companions was a sore trial to us, which may have been the reason why we were so content to play with one another.

We always knew what we wanted to be when we grew up, although it changed from time to time. For a while I was going to be a nurse, of course, and then an actress, and then a singer—but always a writer. While you, early on, were determined to be a doctor. I still laugh when I think about it—and how good it is to be able to laugh now, however briefly. Mother was ill, and our beloved Doctor Dan came to see her. You were sitting on the porch steps with a naked doll, which had a high-ridge papier-maché body, on your lap. You were so bent over your patient that you didn't see him coming.

"And what are you doing, my dear?" Doctor Dan inquired, pausing beside you.

You barely looked up. "I'm operating on Susie," you said briefly.

"Oh?" the doctor inquired. "What are you operating for?"

"I'm taking her backbone out of her front and putting it in her back where it belongs," you told him.

The doctor nodded. "Very wise," he said, and hurried upstairs to hide his mirth and to tell Mother she had a potential surgeon on her hands.

But along with wanting to be a doctor you always wanted to be an artist, and when I wrote my deathless verse in one of Father's discarded notebooks, you drew pictures on top of them. This, I felt, was carrying things too far, but at the time you were stronger muscularly than I was, so I searched for a compromise. "Very well," I remember saying in a haughty voice, "when I'm grown up I will write books and you will illustrate them." "All right," you said promptly, which made me wonder how seriously you took my dictum, but, as it turned out, that is exactly what happened . . . for a time.

I always loved to watch the sureness with which you drew. From the very beginning, when you had coloring books, you stayed within the line, and while that's true of many children and cannot be considered remarkable, the thing that pointed out that you would become an artist was your dissatisfaction with that sort of childish art, and going off on your own. You scorned copying anything and when you were art judge for would-be artists in Girl Scouts you refused to let them copy anything, either. I should amend that, however. You did copy three of Vermeer's paintings, because you wanted to find out how he achieved such brilliance with such a low-key palette. And you found out, and sold two of the copies to the chairman of the Philadelphia Art Museum, while you hid the third one for yourself and wouldn't even bring it out for eleven years! Now, of course, it hangs on our living-room wall, the lamp underneath casting just the right light up onto the canvas, and everyone who sees it exclaims over it.

You always worked with amazing speed, because you knew exactly what you wanted to achieve and were able to go about it without any fumbling. I relished the story of how you persuaded the director of the Mauritshuis to let you copy Vermeer's Lezende Vroutje. He was polite and oh, so regretful. "We only allow one artist in the cabinet where a particular painting hangs," he explained, "and an American artist is due here to copy that painting next week."

"Then may I have this week?" you asked, and he said, in astonishment,

"You may have permission, of course, Juffrouw, but you could not possibly do it in a week."

"Will you let me try?" you said and he bowed.
"The cabinet is yours. I only hope you will not be disappointed or will not say that I did not warn you."

And you copied it in five furious sessions . . . . . a lovely thing. I think even Vermeer would have been proud of you.

Those deft hands could do so much. I admired and envied you always. My knitting was adequate and I liked doing the plainest of things—bandages for lepers, Red Cross sweaters, scarves for seamen. But you reveled in the 12-row patterns, and could tell at a glance whether you were on row eight or nine, while if I tried a four-row one I generally had to ask you to extricate me from a knitter's nightmare. You embroidered exquisitely, where I could never stay within the blue printed outlines. You crocheted intricate bootees and caps, you did Elizabethan blackwork and managed to talk while you counted threads. You did lovely silk screens, and all I was good for was to hang the prints up to dry. You created wood-carvings and executed them, you invented your own designs for needlepoint and petit point—everywhere I look there is some reminder of your work—and batik, which intrigued you after we had been out to the Netherlands East Indies. You did water-colors and gouaches and oils and dry point and gesso and pen-and-inks and scratchboards which went on exhibitions and won prizes—you were still in your twenties when you were included in Who's Who in Art. But I could only do pottery.

"Try it," I urged, thinking what fun it would be to work together in our craft room.

"Too soft," you said. "I like harder materials."

You wove me chenille evening bags, and material for a suit, and lovely scarves, and made Mother table doilies and bureau runners. You made everyone afghans of scraps of colored wool—no two squares alike, in some of them, just to see whether you could have that many color combinations. You studied silver and gold jewelry work—by yourself, of course!—and I can still see you, your cheeks puffed out from blowing on the pipe to solder, your face getting redder and redder because it wasn't quite right yet and you would not stop blowing, though I was afraid you'd have a stroke. You made me silver rings, set with beach stones and semi-precious stones, you made me a gold bracelet and gold earrings, as a Christmas present, and because I had a habit of popping into your studio during the daytime, you worked on them at night and had them ready for me Christmas morning.

Your creativity seemed endless, and your joy in it was a beautiful thing to see. I often think—and we often spoke of it, too—that if children could be encouraged to express their creativity, in whatever form it took, from the earliest time on, as we were encouraged, there would not be the restlessness and the vandalism and the crime that there is now. You cannot create something, however amateurish and misshapen and crude it is, without a sense of holiness. Lo and behold, this I have wrought! It is exciting and humbling at the same time. It is what young people need, for having felt that exaltation and humility they could not destroy someone else's work.

Tom-Tom is tired of chasing imaginary butterflies and is standing up, his paws on my lap, his liquid brown eyes beseeching me. I must take him for a walk, since it is exactly three-thirty and his time sense is flawless.

We will go up the hill, while he sniffs at all the old places and searches out some new ones and hunts non-existent bones and pretends other dogs are lurking behind the flowering bushes, and then we will come down the hill again and go over to the pond and watch the ducks gliding gracefully under the drooping willow branches. When you were ill you would say, "Have a good time. And come back soon. I'll be waiting for you."

Oh, dear God, how I wish you were waiting for me now!

August

Dear Toley,

Of all the nicknames you had, you liked Toto best, of course, but Toley, I think, came next. You loved your own name, but it was hard—sometimes impossible—to get people to say Cateau with the accent in the right place since it was spelled Cato. You objected to being called *Ca*to, like the Roman censor, and it was a grim battle to get Miss W. in history class to call you properly.

"*Ca*to," she would say, "bound the peninsula of India." And you would say, "My name is Ca*to*, Miss W."

"Oh yes, Ca*to*. Well, *Ca*to, bound the peninsula. . . ."

"My name is Ca*to*, Miss W."

"I know. I must remember."

But next day it was the same thing, and the next, and the next, but you, with your determined little chin lifted, would not answer until she said it correctly. You won, in time. That bout, however, decided you to change the spelling to the French form . . . . and oddly enough, after that, you had no trouble with anyone!

Your first name, though, was nothing to the difficulties we both had with our last name. No one—except a Hollander—was able to say it right just by looking at it, and if they heard it they could never spell it from what they heard. Mother said that after she married she began making a list of the mis-spellings that came on letters and got to fifty-seven in a few weeks and then stopped. It would have been interesting to see how many changes could have been rung on those seven letters. "D—e," you told someone as a child, "capital L and seven wiggles." It was as good a way as any of getting over the hurdle. Then, as we grew older, we had the problem of deciding whether it should be written with a small or a large d. Father always used the large, and you opted for that, too, but I could never make up my mind whether I liked the appearance of the d better as a small or large letter. I used one and sometimes the other, and it's rather fun now to look over our row of books and see the variations—even to the closeness of the *de* to the rest of the name! Naturally we were cataloguers' despair, but it did get us attention from them and from librarians when we went to conventions!

You never thought you could write. You could *tell* a story, yes, you said, and plots seemed to spring fullblown from that head of yours. You told them beautifully and interestingly—our long practice with our home-made soap opera stood us in good stead when I corralled you to join me in the story hours I started at the Library.

What a stimulating experience that was! Two hundred children sitting on the floor in front of us in the old art gallery, inching forward as the story got exciting, faces upturned, mouths open, eyes large and shining. When you drew the princess or the wicked grandmother or the fire-belching dragon before their very eyes on the blackboard their attention was hypnotic. And afterward they would dash down the stairway, clattering like a horde of ponies into the children's room where I had gathered books with the same kind of stories in them, and descend on the aged librarian with "I want this!" "Gimme this one!" "Here's my card—where's the Yellow Fairy Book?" The books would disappear—and the children, in time—but the librarian couldn't take it. After some weeks of that she asked to be transferred to cataloguing which was carried on in the cool, quiet basement.

It was that story-telling experience, however,

that probably set us on our course. It's interesting now to look back and see how it all built up over the years and to see what part fate played in it—if one wants to call it fate. You were set on an art career, I was doing stories, articles, interviews, poems for magazines and newspapers. Then you went to Paris—of course, an artist had to go to Paris—and while you were there I sent out some of your poems which were accepted, to your vast amazement. But it didn't change you yet. After your return you set up in a studio in New York. Those were fun times, because I had a place to stay overnight after a round of theaters and ballets, and you were next to the Pen and Brush, our beloved club, and we could go there twice a week for programs and exhibits.

But the Depression came and people weren't handing out art work except to the well-knowns, nor spending money on having their portraits painted, in spite of the rave reviews you had from major critics. Sadly you gave up the studio and fixed up one on the third floor of our Mansard. It was then, in this lean art period, that I asked why you didn't write. I reminded you of your story mind and your flair for dialogue and your ability to keep the listener listening, which should work the same way to keep the reader reading.

"I simply can't write longhand," you said. "It

infuriates me, its's so slow and I would lose the whole flow of the story. Besides, I'm an artist."

But I persisted and finally you said, "Well, if I borrow your typewriter I'll do three stories, and if I sell one for enough to buy myself a typewriter I may consider it."

You sold the first one, and you had to buy the typewriter. After that, it was smooth sailing for me. I had won my point. And you were literally 'hooked' on writing. "It's certainly easier on the feet," you said wryly.

Still, it was obvious that you looked back, quite often, to those days in Paris with a real sense of nostalgia. It was your first experience away from home and family and you had to make your way in a foreign country, from finding a place to live to learning how to take the so-called compliments of girl-watchers along the boulevards. I remember one letter you wrote saying in triumph, "I know I have really mastered French now—I bested a taxi-driver in an argument." Nobody in France would believe you were American. You were Spanish or Dutch or Belgian or Swiss, because between Uncle Henri's and Father's tutelage your French was absolutely un-American!

It was a dreadfully hot summer when you were away, and we loved your description of serving ice cream in cantaloupe halves to your French artist-landlady, Mlle. B.

"She looked at it horror, and then threw up her hands. 'Comme c'est bizarre!' " she cried, and waited for me to writhe in pain because I was actually eating it."

I was stewing in our airy bedroom at home, turning out copy and trying to forget my loneliness. And looking foward to the time we'd be together over there in the fall, when the family decided to pick you up before we did another leisurly tour of Europe. You were on the quay waiting for us when the ship docked at LeHavre. I spotted you first and then cast a quick look at Mother. When she saw you she drew in her breath. "It can't be!" she said. But it was. You had cut you hair in page-boy with bangs, and you wore a bright lipstick and a beret. I really thought Mother was about to faint. "How she's changed," she said sadly, biting her lip. Father put his arm around her. "People do change," he reminded her gently. "And she's still our very special Toto."

I thought the whole effect quite ravishing and wished I had the courage to do something like that. The return to bangs went back to your childhood, I recognized, and I think Mother did, too. You alway liked them and determined to have them yourself, so one day at school you took your scissors, grabbed a bunch of hair and snipped across your forehead. The effect was startling and rather raggedy, and Mother was horrified.

"Who did that?" she demanded indignantly when you came home. This was your first—and last—attempt at cover-up. You could tell from her tone of voice that something boded ill, as they say.

"Emma—Sickels," you came out with.

"A *very* appropriate name," Mother commented. "What does she look like?"

"She's—she's sort of pale."

"I should think she would be, doing a thing like that. Where does she sit?"

"In back of me."

"How could she cut your hair sitting in back of you?"

"She—she—was going down the aisle and took her scissors and—just cut them."

"And what did the teacher say to all this?"

The questions came on inexorably. Mother's nine years of teaching school stood her in good stead in the grilling.

How often we laughed at the episode afterward! The questions every day . . . What did Emma wear? What does her father do? Does her mother ever come to school? What did she have in her lunch box this morning? You grew so terribly tired of making up stories to cover the previous stories—even you, who loved making things up!—that you wished the whole thing would end. But you never wished you hadn't cut the bangs!

Finally one day Mother said quietly, "Cateau, who *did* cut your hair?" and you gave a great sigh and said, "I did." The relief was tremendous. The subterfuge and the constant invention and the checking on yourself to see if the stories still meshed was over, at last. "I thought so," Mother said. "Get me my hairbrush."

That horrifying experience effectively put an end to any further fibbing. From then on you were fantastically truthful in daily life, leaving made-up stories and their consequences entirely to your fiction. Interestingly enough, nothing was ever said about the incident again, and Mother let you keep the bangs, after having them professionally trimmed.

They lasted for years, and then you were in for a Clèo de Merode hair-do and then various kinds of permanents, and you had a particularly effective one when you left for Paris. I suppose that was what startled Mother when she saw you. But, come to think of it, you hadn't really changed. You had simply reverted.

You were always much more willing to try something new, however, than I was. It took you years of persistence and cajolery to get me to cut my hair, and to buy an electric typewriter—you had had one for years—

and to get away from certain colors in clothing that I thought were most suitable. You were always right, of course, and I never resented the fact that you were. With your artist's eye you knew instinctively what was effective for me—"Nothing frilly," you said, "heavy materials— orange, ruby-red, emerald green, tailored things for everyday"—and once I tried your suggestions I was quickly convinced. It was getting me to make the changes that wore you out, you said. And when you designed dresses for me and had them made up I felt like a very superior princess. When people said, "Where did you get that stunning evening gown?" I could hardly keep from smirking as I said, "Cateau designed it."

Designing clothes might have been another career for you. You were doing it as a child when we got out our monthly magazine called, modestly, "Inspirations." I was looking through some of the copies the other day— copies that I typed and for which you had to do the illustrations separately for every copy sold (ten cents per)— and even now they are surprisingly modern and effective. You got together a portfolio of your designs, after you had studied designing in New York, and took them around to Seventh Avenue shops.

The experience was revelatory and disheartening. You'd come home evening after evening and tell what had happened. "He said my things were too far ahead of the trend," was one comment you heard over and over. "Six months from now, maybe, but right now nothing doing." Or "He took a few of my sketches and went into a back room and I could hear two men talking and after just enough time had elapsed for one or the other to have copied the sketches he would come out and hand them back. 'Pretty nice, kid. Can't use these, but come back later.' " That taught you, at least, not to let them out of your possession.

But the whole picture was depressing and, to a certain extent, degrading. You had to be tough in that game, it seemed, and you weren't cut out for that kind of toughness. It was nice, however, to be able to do your own designs, and make them up as well, and having learned how to cut and drape on the figure I always loved to hear you tell someone in the alternations department of the store, "If you lift the shoulder here and take it in a bit at the neck," and see their startled look and hear they say, "You're right, but how did you know?"

Part of the fun of living in Paris was having gowns designed for *you.* Of course it was by one of the small couturières hidden away on the third floor of a side street, but a marvel of ability at that. That black lace floor length— which was so effective with your Spanish shawl—was good for twenty years, still in style and still getting compliments. You often wondered, though, what had happened to the 'little couturière' herself and to the pale-faced, scrawny messenger girl who delivered it that night in time for a party.

Paris, for you, was full of stories, because it was full of people, and if you could not hear their stories you made them up. The Russian emigrée who smoked endlessly and had a 'boy friend' who seemingly bought her paintings, and who lived with a house full of cats in the row of villas where you had your studio. The fat concierge who could swear like a trooper, but who always had a soft spot in her heart for you and who would call out when you came home from the Opera at one o'clock, "Are you all right? Did you have a good time?" The woman who ran the triperie where you bought food for your Tigris, the gray kitten which adopted you and lived in your pear tree. The stout cleaning woman whose husband was a chef and who could not come on Mondays because that was his day off and he liked her home cooking. The lovely, sultry-looking young artist, Clare Newberry, who had the apartment above you and with whom you shared wine and cauliflower and letters from home and who was just beginning to make her name as the famous cat portraitist and whose own story was material for half a dozen books. The Lesbian writers and the homosexual men who frequented the Dome and who came and went in your row of villas behind the high iron wall. The croquis classes at L'Academie de la Grande Chaumière, and the male models you hired there to pose for you at your studio. "Do you have good legs?" you reported asking, and half a dozen of them promptly dropped their trousers. You said, with a chuckle that was apparent in your writing. "It was all most businesslike."

Reading over those Parisian letters is like living your experiences over again with you . . . . the excitement of discovering the blue stained glass perfection in the little chapel of Ste. Chappelle; the sampling of restaurants on the Ile de la Cité; the heady diet of theatres and operas and ballets; the visits with new friends and the forcing of your vocabulary to discuss philosophy and art in French; the triumph of finding your way in the Metro; lovely after-noons among the bookstalls; the drenching of your artistic soul in the museums; the unusual tours with the professor and a small band of enthusiasts to the fabulous estates of the landed gentry, with your own private bus, and tea at tucked-away inns. It's all there and your delight in every new experience bubbles up from the airmail paper, with words left out here and there because your pen could not keep up with your racing mind.

When we came to pick you up you were the

perfect guide, for though we had known Paris before, you now knew it intimately and with pride you took us to eating places we had only read about and to small galleries we had not even heard of and to bargains in small shops and to concerts we might have missed. There was a new assurance about you, too, as a result; you had learned to live alone and to rely on yourself, and it was very becoming. *

I'll put the letters back in their folder now. So many memories came flooding over me that it was quite overwhelming, but really a happy experience. I could never destroy letters—the files are bulging with communications from friends and foes and inbetweens, and someday I suppose I will have to do something about it, or my heirs will. But letters from the family were sacred and special, and it is amazing how many things become vivid again when they're taken out and re-read. We were all good letter writers, if I do say so with a certain amount of immodesty. It was a way of visiting, or sharing, and we didn't stint on expressing ourselves.

As children we were delighted with Father's delicious letters in rhyme from wherever he happened to be, and the only reason we could console ourselves when he had to be away on a consulting trip was the fact that every day there would be a special letter for each of us, telling in jouncy, bouncy, humorous rhyme just what he had been doing. Sometimes he wrote one of them in simple Dutch, and if it was too much for us—as it generally was—we had to wait till he came home to translate it for us. Of course we always felt that whatever was written in that tongue had special meaning. Those simple little notes were our sole introduction to his native tongue, except for the nursery rhymes he taught us. I can still recite "Torrentje, torrentje bussekruit, wat kommt heruit," and see you and Father building the tower with your hands, there at the table, and the hands flying apart, accompanied by your shouts of glee when the final line came, "Torrentje is gebroken!"

It probably wasn't awfully good preparation for our subsequent stays, months at a time, in Holland, but perhaps it did in a way predispose us to the language and give us a feeling for it. At least, we weren't afraid to tackle complex things like ordering a spool of thread or asking which tram took us to the Rijksmuseum!

Of course any foreigner who attempts a phrase or two in Dutch is encouraged almost to foolhardiness. "What excellent Dutch you speak!" the astonished natives say. And so you keep trying—which, after all, is how one learns a language. Going to the movies was like a speed-reading course. I'll never forget our first one—a French film, in which the characters spoke French, with subtitles in Dutch, which we had to translate into English, and the tri-lingual feat left us breathless and bleary-eyed.

How could I forget the phrase we learned from

34

Father first of all? "Goede nacht, lieves kind. Wel te rusten."

So, putting aside those dear letters, I say it now to you. Goede nacht, lieves kind. Wel te rusten.

September

Dear Birthday Child,

I've chosen this day on which to write because it is special. Birthdays, thank goodness, in our family were always very special and not just to the celebrant. You and I had a hard time understanding our friends, fortunately only two of them, who never celebrated natal days because, they said, they weren't important, one day was like another. We had an even harder time comprehending the philosophy back of our housekeeper's remark that she never gave or wanted to receive birthday presents . . . the day you were born had no significance, it was the day you died and went on to Paradise that mattered. To each his own, but we were old-fashioned enough to believe in birthdays and to give them all due pomp and circumstance.

Even so, certain ones stand out. When you were very small you were the recipient of a miracle. Anyhow, you though it was one and you thought it for years. While your guests were inside, fishing for presents in the wishing well—which was the bottom of the hall rack—Father came home and tied balls made to look like very realistic apples on the two catalpa trees in the back garden. Then Mother said, "Why don't you all go out to play while I get the refreshments?" And out you all tumbled, to be struck dumb by the metamorphosis of the catalpas, which only half an hour ago had been just branches and leaves.

There was a ball for each child, all on sufficiently long strings so that the guests could grab them, and it was only a trice before the trees were denuded of their fruit. At dinnertime you told Father a wide-eyed, breathless story of the miraculous apples. "How did it happen?" you demanded. "They weren't there before."

"Who knows?" Father said seriously. "Anything is possible on a birthday."

All ordinary chores were suspended for the day, and you got to choose exactly what you'd like to have for dinner. No matter how outrageous or contrary to the best nutritional diet, you had it. Yours varied from year to year, but the desert was invariably the same—caramel cake with caramel icing. The housekeeper always groaned when she heard it, for she hated to caramelize sugar, and I don't blame her. One year I said I'd do it, and I understood her objections even better. Eventually we discovered Mrs. H. who loved to make cakes and made superb ones, and after that, when a call came to her around the 22nd, she always said brightly, "I suppose you want another caramel cake?"

When we lived in the Big House, special dinners generally gave way to corn roasts. They were immensely popular with all our friends and most of them didn't hesitate to ask in August if they were to be invited to the roast in September. There was always little individual steaks—filet mignon if Mother felt expansive—and tomatoes from the garden and piles and piles of corn on the cob, freshly husked.

The current chauffeur was delegated to cut branches from the privet hedge and fashion sharp-pointed sticks from them. Father had built a simple but most effective grill out of bricks in the garden under the giant elm, garden chairs and benches were put in a circle, a card table was spread with the food, the fire had been lighted a strategic time before, and the guests each speared a cob and took turns, three at a time, holding it in and over the flames till it charred deliciously. Spread with butter there was no finer eating, everyone said. I can still remember Mrs. B., who was the chaperone of the club we belonged to, putting a hand on her ample middle and groaning, "I simply cannot eat another bite . . . not another bite . . . but I must have one more cob." It was the better part of valor not to count how many she had had or we would have really worried.

When twilight fell and the mosquitoes began to appear we went inside, and there was ice cream and the inevitable caramel cake ablaze with candles. You always managed to blow them out with one try.

And then, of course, there were the verses. That was really the best part. Scrapbook after scrapbook here on the shelves hold some of the verses—not all, for many were lost over the years. There had to be a verse for everything—a pencil required a verse as well as a ring, a box of candy required versifying as much as a satin slip. They were fun to do. We tried to outdo each other in rhymes and wit and nonsense and hidden meanings. The birthday child had to read them aloud—before or after opening the present was always specified, so that there could be no anticlimax.

To cap it all there was a long screed in verse for the Child herself or himself. Here was a chance for the rest of us to get things off our chests, to make fun of pecadilloes, to spoof a current fad or mannerism, and to offer advice which, if taken, would have definitely spoiled the whole upcoming year.

You often complained, in a way that I refused to take to heart, that my birthdays frequently were spent abroad or on the high seas, whereas in September we always seemed to be at home. I noticed that you had a thoroughly good time at those 'at home' parties, but of course I *could* see the advantage of a maitre d' having a menu specially printed for your birthday dinner, and to have the waiters bring in bowls of caviar and a cake decorated with cherries and angelica to simulate the carnelian necklace I'd just been given. Father was very good at arranging these things.

He was good at so many things, wasn't he? A truly Renaissance Man, his abilities and interests far-ranging. A mathematical wizard, an electrical and mechanical engineer, an inventor, a gardener, a wood-carver, a story-teller and wonderful teacher, someone who could make the most abstruse scientific subject simple and clear, a singer—in his early days—and one who never let a day go by without sitting down at the piano or organ and improvising the most delightful melodies. I can still see you as a child, dancing to his playing, and I always liked the story that he and Mother played duets, with me slung in a hammock between dining-room and living room, until I cried out in protest.

There wasn't anything we couldn't ask him—and get an answer that satisfied and enlighted us. And he had the most wonderful sense of humor, quiet to the point of being dead-pan sometimes, but gentle and perceptive and with an unexpected play on words. Punning became a family pastime; no matter how people deride it, we adored it, and many a dinner was enlivened by each one trying to outdo the other.

I pity young people who haven't had the stimulus of fun at the dinner table. We talked of anything and everything, and you, whose seat was nearest the library, were generally delegated to hunt a word in the dictionary if there was any dispute about it. We had evenings when we were supposed to speak only French, and others when German was the rule, and though we first tried to get away with simple sentences like "Pass the butter, please," we were drawn out to tell of our daily happenings and anything that interested us. The French and German evenings were fairly silent, just the same, for a good many years, and we saved all the exciting and complicated events for the nights when we could speak English.

On Sundays there were long walks , when Father made a point of correcting the garbled Bible stories we had heard in the morning—our teachers were often young girls who apparently had just read the lesson before they came to head the class and weren't any too sure of the tale themselves—and after he had set us straight we would ramble through the woods and down by the river or along the creek, stopping to examine flowers and weeds and birds' nests and lichens under the ever-present magnifying glass. One thing would lead to another, and we came home filled with stories of chemistry and history and star-lore, and always with a bouquet of wilting wild flowers for Mother.

Long before Rachel Carson he instilled in us a sense of wonder, and a desire to know as much as we could know of the world and the things in it. That was his intangible gift to us, but I think the tangible gift that made the most lasting impression on you—and me—was the doll house he built for us.

It wasn't a secret. It couldn't be, because he had to use the big work table in the basement and every night he disappeared down cellar and we could hear hammering and sawing and, on occasions, we were invited down to inspect the progress.

We disposed of so many childhood treasures in the course of years, but the doll house was never to be parted with, though some of the furniture disappeared. It was a little masterpiece, really, with an elevator in which the dolls could be moved from one story to another, with a paneled dining-room that had a fireplace and a window-seat, and inscribed over the doorway of the pillared portico, "Villa Cadelto." That impressed us mightily—the combination of our names into the name of this fabulous house! You wove rugs on your first hand loom and I made curtains for the windows, and the family of dolls rode up and down in the elevator until they must have been dizzy.

It is still here. We had such plans for renovating it, and we did arrange between ourselves that we would give each other birthday presents of furniture for the house, expensive and well-crafted furniture that would do the house proud. So there it is now, with its pewter chandelier and its Empire beds and the brass fender for the fireplace and the tiny dishes on the table and the standing lamps near the upholstered chairs and the handsome secretary made by Mr. R., the cabinet maker, full of infinitesimal books. And I can't bear to go down and look at it anymore.

While Father was making the doll house Grandmother was upstairs sewing on the silk patchwork quilts she was doing for our beds. If ever people were blessed, we were blessed to have had Grandmother come to live with us for seven years. You were too young to remember her house and extraordinary garden, but I recall going there often with Mother, and coming home always with bouquets of flowers and bags of fresh vegetables.

She could make anything grow. People brought

her their sick plants and asked if she could do something with them, and she always did. "But what did you do?" they would inquire incredulously. "I loved them," she would answer. I can see her now, in our home, with the wire stand by the window full of plants in all stages of green and flowering . . . . and all of them healthy. She would have on a big apron and in her lap one of the pots. She would take off the dead leaves and aerate the soil and pour water on from the little brass watering can . . . . and then, with a pat, set it back in its place among the others. Loving them was right . . . . she loved them into doing their best for her.

We spent many happy hours in her room, sitting at her feet, listening to stories of her young life, or learning to sew. She was the epitome of patience with us—you took to the art quickly and deftly—but between my aversion to the whole process and my left-handedness, I was something of a problem. She would look down at me, stretching my arms as far as possible before cutting off the thread and say gently, "A short thread, my dear, will not tangle. Cut it off here," pointing to a place about a third down the line. Or she would come to stand in back of me, in order to find out how I was doing with that left-handed awkwardness. But she did not try to change me, and for that I was grateful.

44

When we tired of sewing, I was allowed to arrange the buttons in her button bag and you would do her hair. Poor darling Grandmother! An angel of forebearance! Maybe because you were named for her she saw you with a special pride and anything you did to her was all right, including parting her hair into at least a hundred separate strands and making pigtails out of all of them. When you showed her your handiwork in a mirror, she would laugh. "I'm glad I don't have to go out," she would say merrily.

Her lap was ample and comfortable, and with your head on her breast you would be quiet for an hour at a time. There was complete understanding between you, and she showed her love in many ways.

The one I remember best is when you had decided to bake some cupcakes. It was a simple recipe, called "Delicious," and in fact the cook had made them often and they *were* delicious. Your effort this time turned out spectacularly well. The cakes rose beautifully and browned to an appetizing brown. You were proud enough to burst. You put three of them on a little plate and started up the stairway to show Grandmother. But half way up you tripped in your haste and fell down. The cupcakes rolled over the steps, the plate broke, and you burst into tears.

Grandmother came running. "What is it, darling?"

"The cup—the cup—the cupcakes!" you hiccoughed.

Grandmother took in at a glance what had happened—the broken plate, the tender cakes in pieces. "Never mind," she said firmly, "pick them up, dear, and bring them here to me."

Which you did. And she ate every one, crumbs, dust and all. "They are *really* delicious!" she cried and gave you a tremendous hug. I often think it's not the big crises of life that you remember so well as the little things, and this is one picture that stayed with both of us over the years.

You offered the same kind of ego-bolstering comfort to me. I had never made anything more than doll clothes, but suddenly I decided it would be fun to make a dress for you. After all, I would prove to Grandmother that her efforts were not in vain. Unbeknownst to anyone I went down town and bought several yards of blue-and-white and pink-and-white checked gingham. While I was about it, I thought, I might as well make two dresses instead of one. We had a playroom on the third floor and there I would repair, lock the door, and go about my business. When you knocked and demanded entrance I muttered between the pins in my mouth (a forbidden thing, by the way), "Go away—it's a surprise." The cutting out didn't prove difficult—I did just what I'd done for doll clothes, doubled the material, cut short sleeves as an extension of the shoulders, slashed a Vee for the neck hole—and presto, sewed up the side seams and did the hem. In short order they were done, and I pressed them and presented them to you with a nonchalant, "I thought maybe you'd like a couple of new dresses."

You were open-mouthed and almost speechless. "For me?" you shrieked finally. "You made these for *me*?"

I nodded and watched you try them on. Miraculously, they fit, if you could call the sack-like effect a fit. You pranced in front of the mirror. "I love pink—I love blue—I love *you*," you caroled and gave me a bear hug.

What's more, you wore them. You wore them to Mother's dismay, day after day, insisting that they be laundered so you could wear them again. You wore them to school and to neighborhood parties in spite of Mother's pleas. "Why not wear that embroidered voile I bought you, dear?" "I like these," you insisted. And you wore them until you outgrew them which, to Mother's relief, was shortly.

But what you did for me was an everlasting blessing. You gave me uncritical love in return for my bumbling effort to please. And no one could have asked for more.

That love never failed me.

October

Dear Jessica Lyon and Kay Hamilton,

Every night for the past several weeks I have been taking down one of your books and reading through it. It's a deeply emotional experience and one which I wasn't willing to have until now. Even so, though I thought I was ready, I find myself wiping away tears because I am so moved. I can hear you in page after page, hear you talking, hear you chuckling, recognize your turn of phrase and your delight in your more talkative or eccentric characters. I am aware again, in admiration, of your handling of specific theme, how cleverly you invented your people to carry it out and how fair you were to them, letting them work out their problems in a logical, revealing way.

It's small wonder that they found their way into

the hearts of so many young people—and adults—and someday I will go over the file of letters from people who were moved to write to you. But not now.

Your two pen names stood you in good stead. For one thing, they were far simpler than your real name! I never got around to an alias. And I was really touched when you decided to go into novels for young adults and would not have them published under Cateau deLeeuw because, as you said, I was already established and you didn't want to ride into success on my coat-tails. Still, Lyon is a form of deLeeuw, so you weren't that far away from me at that. And Kay Hamilton came into being because Kay stood for Catherine, which is really Cateau, and Hamilton was the place where we were born. The funny part is there was already a woman writing under the name of Kay Hamilton—fashion articles, as I recall—and after she got into correspondence with you, you became fast friends.

People always ask, How long does it take you to write a book? (I still get the question whenever I appear before clubs or schools.) But when you would say, "I've done a full-length novel in twenty-nine hours!" the gasp that would go through the audience was spontaneous and incredulous. Twenty-nine hours! How could you? they implied. And afterward they would come up and ask you to enlarge on that amazing statement.

But I knew it was true, and with considerable amusement you would try to tell them how you did it. It was when you said, "I use the subconscious," that the mystery deepened.

I suppose people who never use it will never understand how anyone else uses it. It has certainly been the subject of countless conversations with people who want the mystery explained, yet we could count on one hand the number who actually tried it out. However, when we did the book based on habits and made that the climax section, our response from unknown readers was tremendous and very gratifying. In other words, I imagine, those who really wanted it to work for them were willing to go about cultivating it.

It was a wonderful time saver for us—and still is for me. When we got into the rhythm of doing a short short every day, I would say to you at night, "I'll need a plot tomorrow morning," and you would say, "Okay" and tell your subconscious to come up with one, and roll over and go to sleep. Promptly at ten next morning, when I sat down at the typewriter, you had the plot ready for me.

That was really the beginning of our conscious and deliberate use of the subconscious. I suppose we picked up the idea of using our Subby, as we called it, from Father, although he never spoke of it. We simply saw the result of his ability to tell himself what he wanted to do, and when he wanted to do it, and when he wanted it completed. How often we watched, from the living-room windows, as he marched around our 90-foot porch, smoking a cigar and thinking something out. And when he stopped to wave the lighted end in a triumphant arc, we knew he had it. In our earlier years we took this sort of thing for granted, but later on we got curious and asked just how he went about solving a problem or inventing a machine to do a job which had never been done before. His explanation was, then, the foundation of the use of the subconscious which we cultivated in ourselves. "I find out everything I can from existing sources about the problem I'm to solve; then I discard everything I know about the present difficulties; then I start from scratch and invent a machine which will do what has to be done."

It sounded so simple . . . . and of course it was. When we did stories and, later on, books, we used the same basic idea—with slight differences. We consciously did all our research for a particular story, especially when it was laid in another time, we got all our necessary information together, we told ourselves when we wanted to begin, and how long the books should be, and when we wanted it finished, and then we sat down at our IBM's with a mind clear of everything but the flow from brain to paper, and let ourselves go. That was one reason you were able to do a novel in twenty-nine hours, and why we never missed a deadline.

Perhaps it sounds egotistical as I write it down this way, but really it is such a boon that you and I both tried to convert others to the system, and it's why I rather enjoy just writing out the process again. One of the amusing parts of our lectures was when, inadvertently, we mentioned our use of the subconscious, and without exception someone would pipe up, in the middle of the talk or immediately afterward, "Tell us about the subconscious!"

Then we lit into it, and there they sat, fairly open-mouthed and incredulous. But how many followed through we never knew—except from occasional phone calls and letters that came to us because of our book on the subject. We did know a half a dozen cases where using the subconscious, for those particular people, was a kind of life saver, and that should be our reward, perhaps. Even if there had been only one case where someone had a new lease on his creative life, or had learned to use his time more effectively, or had developed a new set of habits through the use of the subconscious, should have heartened us . . . and did.

I always got a chuckle out of your reply to people who persisted in knowing how you achieved so much in such a little time. "I work in the trance state," you would say matter-of-factly. That really got them! "The trance state!" they would repeat in disbelief. "You mean you're hypnotized?" "To a certain extent," you would reply, equally solemnly. "But how do you get into it—and who takes you out?" "I get myself in," you answered, and your eyes would begin to twinkle, "and when I'm ready I get myself out." Almost from the beginning of these questions we realized that there was no use explaining what you actually meant, and if people wanted to believe you hypnotized yourself, let them.

I think we both never failed to warn people about the work that had to be done consciously—and this was the part no one wanted to believe. The other end of the proposition sounded so alluring—just sit there, with your mind clear, and let the words come out of your fingers onto the paper! You couldn't convince them of the hours you spent at the library, of the books you bought or got on loan—from anywhere from Trenton to Philadelphia to Montclair to the Library of Congress—and read. You couldn't make them believe in the thousands of words of notes you took—until we got the idea of taking along those voluminous loose-leaf binders to prove what we said. Children were more impressed than adults. "One hundred thousand words of notes," you told them, "for a twenty-eight thousand word book"—holding up the notes and the finished book. But even so, it was hard for them to take it in.

I was always grateful for the fact that you loved the note-taking and the endless reading and the researching in obscure volumes and the need to pursue an elusive fact for months, if you had to, just for the satisfaction of having it absolutely correct. Because then I could make use of all your work in my own writing!

"How do you collaborate?" people invariably asked us. "Do you write together, and how do you decide who writes what?" "When we do a book together," you would tell them, "as a rule I do the research and the plotting and hand it over to Adèle who does the writing." Lucky me! But interestingly enough, in the one book we actually wrote together, it is now impossible to tell which person wrote which part. I suppose that's an example of having rapport . . . and in how many ways we had it!

This ability to get into each other's minds—and hearts—was what made our life together so satisfying. We knew what the other one was thinking; we could—when we were impolite—finish out the other's sentences; we knew, just by looking, when the other one was feeling down or ill or worried. It was never necessary to say, "What's the matter?" We knew.

54

This is one of the hard things I have to bear now. There is no one who reads my thoughts, who sympathizes or rejoices with me as you did. It is a beautiful October day—a blue and gold one, as we always said, and I thought, this is the kind of weather when we would simultaneously stop work and say, "Let's go out for a ride and see the changing of the leaves." But there was no one to say it to. And then the postman came and brought me a letter, a letter I'd been hoping and waiting for, telling me that an editor liked my latest book and wanted to publish it. Instinctively I looked over at the chair where you so often sat, and I opened my mouth to say, "Toto, listen to this!" And there was no one to say it to.

All our adult lives there was that joy of sharing good news and little triumphs. An acceptance, a lecture date, a painting to be exhibited, a poem sold . . . and all the excitement and the thrill has to be self-contained. I come home from a party, spiilling over with news, and there's no one to tell it to. I work toward a goal and achieve it, and there's no one to rejoice with me. Oh, I can tell a friend, and she can say, "How nice!" but that's it. I cannot share the tiny details or go over the long path that led to this delicious moment, or have the feeling that someone deeply cares. The cold truth is driven home once more— no one does care deeply, or ever will again.

November

My Special One:

Rain is sluicing down the windows, the brown leaves are piling in sodden masses against the wall, and Tom-Tom is curled up in a corner plainly saying, "Don't disturb me till this is over."

I'd like to curl up in a corner myself. The November blahs are upon me. I could think I am getting a cold except that by talking sternly to myself I hope to avoid it. Everything aches, and it's not from strenuous exercise. This feeling happens every year at this time and every year I imagine I'm getting the grippe—the old-fashioned word for flu or virus now—and wonder how I can feel so awful and still go walking around.

November is such a busy month to feel so peculiar! We used to wonder if we'd make our lecture dates, and the book-and-author luncheons I had contracted to emcee hung heavily upon me and Book Week loomed ahead with trips out of town and autographing parties. How many times we grimly said, "Mind over matter," and went doggedly ahead. And yet we loved all of it—and I still do. The only trouble was the weather for lecture dates, and for the book-and-author affairs I still have to worry if the authors will be well enough to make it.

Those lecture dates were a story on themselves. I look back now and wonder how we did it. The program chairman, as a rule, had the 'very-little-money-to-work-with-but-you-meet-such-interesting-people' routine, and we learned to bite our tongues before we said, "Then why ask us? And as for interesting people, we know enough of them now." But those dates that actually came through were fun. We generally had to ride fifty to a hundred miles to the club—that is, you had to drive and I merely sat by and tried to be interesting—and then when we got to the clubhouse, whose situation had not been accurately described by the chairman, we had to sit through a business meeting and then meet a stream of people who insisted on asking questions while we set up your portable easel on stage.

Father had made the ingenious contraption out of

two by fours, varnished brown, with butterfly nuts at all points and a shelf to hold the easel and place for a strong light to be placed over it. Assembling it was easy but it did take time. When it was finally set up and we had tested the light, and got a card table for you to put your chalks on, and laid oilcloth under the easel to catch the chalk dust, and washed our hands and straightened our hair, we could relax and listen to endless reports from endless committees.

However, audiences were one of our delights as authors. We learned to test the temper of an audience almost at once. There were the enthusiastic ones—glad to be out, no matter what the talk was about—the testy ones, particularly on bad days, the show-me type who sat in stiff-necked propriety, daring you to be interesting or humorous or both. They were the most fun to wear down. Because we did ensnare them, time and time again. It was like a game with heavy odds against us, and every time we won we could give ourselves a gold star and a brownie. That was the kind of audience that was most vociferous in its applause, most lavish in its praise, and most likely to spend a goodly sum when your pictures were auctioned off afterward.

Driving home, after a tea which we had no time to drink and dismantling the easel and re-packing the car trunk, we would talk over the affair. And chuckle. There was always at least one person who came up and peered intently at the drawing still remaining on the easel and asked, "Where are the pin holes?" "What pin holes?" you would say. "Well, you must have something like that to show you where to draw!" The fact that you did the complete head in full color in two minutes was utterly baffling and of course, they felt, you must have had some hidden guide-lines.

And then there would be the woman who wanted to know if we were really sisters because we seemed to like each other so much and we definitely had no facial resemblance. And there would be the officer of some visiting club who wanted to know our fees and when she heard them would turn away or mutter vaguely about 'you'll hear from me.' Which we never did. And there would be the reporter who would, we knew, misspell our name and get Bali mixed up with the Dutch West Indies. And there would be the spots in our talks where, though we both spoke spontaneously and had no notes, the audience would give a little gasp or laugh out loud or applaud. These reactions came so regularly that we learned to pause in expectation—and were never disappointed.

There were the trips through rainstorms and hail storms and snowstorms, but we always reached home, sometimes drenched, frequently late, but happy and tired, and there was always hot chocolate and little bread and butter sandwiches waiting for us. It was fun to talk it over, to tell our parents of the amusing incidents that had happened, to settle back with the feeling that we had done a good job. And there was the addition to our knowledge of human nature—that it was the same no matter where you went, a thought which comforted us sometimes and dismayed us at others.

The book-and-author luncheons were other occasions on which we were to verify our suspicions about human nature. You were a darling to drive me everywhere, although you did not go for them (after all, I was paid to run them and you just went along for the ride!), but how terribly glad I was that you were along on two occasions when the promised speaker failed to show up and sent no word, and I just called on you to get up and talk about your books or the subconscious or something! And of course you did—and wowed them. You had such a quick-silver mind, and a lovely sense of humor that went with it, and audiences responded to you with delight.

I often thought of the phrase, as you spoke, 'holding them in the hollow of your hand,' which you did. When you were one of the featured speakers at other book-and-author luncheons it was demonstrated time and again. I never had you (except as the last resort) at anything

I presided over. And there was another instance of human nature and ethics. For any number of times people would say, "Why didn't you have your sister? She has a new book out." Or they would ask me why I didn't put myself on the program, since *I* had a new book on the market. They always seemed flabbergasted at my reply, "It wouldn't be ethical." In the beginning that question left *me* flabbergasted, but after a time I began to understand that for many people furthering their own interest, no matter how, is of prime importance.

Year after year, for clubs all over the state, I've presided at these luncheons and I have yet to convince the audience that authors don't get the entire price of their book. It seems incomprehensible to people that if a book sells for $8.95, the author only gets one-tenth of that. You can tell them over and over again, but they still don't take it in. What's more, they fail to comprehend that you don't tote your own books around and sell them and collect the whole price on them—in fact, that you don't tote them period. Why not? they inquire innocently. Or maybe not so innocently, for I don't doubt that many of them would do just that if they were authors.

Being an author is a funny business. At least one must look at it with humor or collapse under the weight of misunderstanding about the profession. How many times we heard, "Are you still writing your little books?" And without waiting for a reply, "Now I have a marvelous story which I want to tell you and you could make it into a book. When could I come up to talk to you?" You'd like to say, "Never," but you are polite and tell the inquirer that you're busy on a couple of stories of your own. "But this is marvelous—really unusual; you've never heard anything like it. It happend to my aunt (or cousin or a friend.)"

This comes to mind because just the other day a man phoned me about the novel he had in mind—I was to write it, of course, and share the profits with him. I repeated my oft-told tale, but it made no difference, he began telling me the plot in such a spate of words and impossible situations that I couldn't get a chance to break in. When he finally paused for a breath I said I didn't want to hear anymore—he must write it himself, at which he said, "Now when we sell it to the movies, how much of it do you want?" I motioned the housekeeper to ring the front door bell and blithely told him someone had come to call and hung up. But I expect the same thing to happen again—as it happened to each of us more times than we cared to count.

Whether we spoke at schools or at sophisticated clubs, the questions people asked were invariably the same. We got a great deal of amusement (sub rosa) out of betting with each other just when the questions would come, but come they would. How long does it take to write a book? How much do you get for it? Where do you get your ideas?

It was that question that always tempted me to say, "At Macy's. $3.44 each, $36.00 a dozen, or $50 a gross." But I never did. Sometimes I really had to bite my tongue. And yet the interest was there and one could not ignore it. To the non-creative person, or at least to the person who does not write, that was always the complete mystery: where do you get your ideas? Futile, really, to tell them that you got them out of your head or from something you read, or from something you saw that started the creative process. It still remained a mystery to them, and from the expression on their faces you knew that they didn't quite believe you; you were just not wanting to give your secret away, they seemed to be thinking. But how do you explain to others where you get your ideas, or what makes them flower into a story or a book?

Still, we knew where we got our ideas, and one of the most fecund places was the Indies. I wonder what would have taken the place of the material we drew from that marvelous trip to Java and Bali and Sumatra so many years ago? I remember, as if it were yesterday, the night Father came home from New York—it was a hot summer day and we were having iced tea on the veranda—and said casually, "How would you like to go to Java?"

We were always traveling somewhere, or planning something, but this was totally unexpected. Father had been to a Java Tiffin Club meeting, I think, and had had his head filled with tales of the glamorous islands from people who lived there. There was no doubt about our response, and it was instant. When would we go? you and I demanded. It would take a year, he explained, to get reservations of cabins with bath on the Dutch ship going out—there weren't that many baths!—and meanwhile we could fill in the time reading about the islands and learning Malay.

The reading was an exciting pleasure; we could hardly wait to see and experience for ourselves. Learning Malay wasn't too difficult, and now we had added to our foreign language dinner table our stumbling efforts to be fluent in Malay. You mastered mata hari sama ham instantly, but said plaintively that you didn't care for fried eggs with ham anyway. Fortunately Malay has no grammar and if you wanted plurals of anything you simply said it twice. "Fine," you commented, "but if I want four chairs I'm not going to sound as if I'm stuttering."

On the ship going out we really had a chance to practice what we'd learned, and some of the results were ludicrous. We had to order from the menu by number, and if we gave the wrong number in Malay we were apt to end up with caviar when we had wanted a grilled lamb chop. But it was an education in itself, and Father got a lot of fun from watching our consternation when the wrong order appeared and we felt compelled to eat it because we couldn't think of the correct number!

It was a time to remember—all of it. We were the only Americans on board, all the other passengers being either Dutch or Indonesian, and the curiosity among them was tremendous. Why were we going out there? On business? Did we own a plantation? Were we in government service? No, we said time and again, we're just going out for pleasure. It was incredible to them . . . . and so, being neophytes they thought it wise to impress on us all the horrors and cautions they could invent. Had we had our shots? No. Were we intent on courting death? Not necessarily, we just didn't think it necessary. Did we know about the various poisons that natives used if they didn't like you? Did we realize we must be careful about the water? Were we going to have a native driver? Then surely we must lock our doors at night or we might lose our valuables and our lives.

There was the other side, too. . . . the lawyers, and doctors, and plantation owners who gave us a balanced picture of life on the islands, the raden and his wife and daughters who gave us our first impression of the dignity and charm of the Javanese people and who became friends with whom we corresponded ever since. Story after story came to light, told with cynicism or romance, and that built up our expectations to a tantalizing degree. Through the Suez and into the Indian Ocean . . . . currant juice at elevenses, dancing at night, curries and exotic dishes, quick, silent little Javanese 'boys' bringing toast and coffee to our cabins in the early mornings, games on deck, and you painting the captain in his cabin for an hour each day for a week.

And then, one day, the engines stopping and in the frightening calm everyone rushing to the rail to see if there was a man overboard. After an interval the engines started again, but there was no explanation—except to you. You had asked to have a photograph made of the portrait, which the captain was purchasing, so that you could have something to show in your album of paintings. And the photographer had complained that he could not do a proper picture with a time exposure because of the throbbing of the engines. So the captain had ordered the engines stopped, for the period required to take a time exposure! It was certainly a first and only, and it was just as well that the passengers didn't know what had happened. The captain seemed quite unconcerned about possible consequences from the company—this was his last trip and he was retiring to the country when he returned to Holland.

Nearing Sumatra we got our first whiff of the orient. There was something in the air, a combination of spices and perfumes and the sense of mystery that floated out to us as we passed silently along the palm-fringed shore.

The islands were everything we had dreamed of, and more. Even now a host of memories flood over me at the mere mention of one of them. The twenty boys with rijst-tafel at the Hotel des Indes. The Chinese merchants squatting in front of us as we sat on the terrace, offering us everything from carved cocoanut shells to filigree silver boxes and begging us to buy so that they could 'go China.' The mosquito netting on the big beds and the houseboys clambering over the sheets swatting flies before they adjusted the netting for the night. Amsah coming every day with the car and taking us to tea plantations and to Borobudur and to Prambanan and to the hill country and to Djockja and Soerabaja and to all the exotic places where we spent the night or the week. Winding roads and little children in abbreviated shirts dancing in the dust; the warong men with their traveling kitchens, and the delicious smells that wafted up from the charcoal fires; the women in their blue and brown sarongs washing linen in the streams as we passed; going to tea in a rich planter's house, with the servants leaving the room, squatting as they backed out. The arrogant Dutch men at hotel dances calling a djongos to light their cigarettes. The big volcanoes with tiny villages up their steep sides; the women planting rice, knee deep in the water, their heads protected by big cone-shaped hats; the terraced rice fields more beautiful than any painting, the scarlet hibiscus flowers falling in the water; the buffaloes plodding along the road, goaded by a stick in the hands of a small boy; sampling the delicious mangosteens and the smelly durians . . . . . oh, the pictures are endless.

You painted madly, and I wrote furiously in notebooks, trying to capture the scenes and the smells and the emotions that welled up on this voyage. At the Sultan's court in Djockja you were the cynosure of all eyes as you sketched the Sultan and his entourage, the musicians in their transparent hats and red and gold uniforms, the procession of the rice bearers and the procession bringing the gold sirih set covered with priceless ikat.

In Bali I Mario posed for you, the most famous dancer of the island going through his incredible dances just for you, stopping in mid-air when you motioned to him and holding the pose like a golden-brown statue until you had sketched it. The old temple guard came to you, too, and posed, and afterward—how well we remembered that and laughed over it every time—he looked at the portrait, gazing at it shaking his head and murmuring, "I never knew I was that small!" For by then you had used all your canvas and all your sketch pads and were reduced to brown paper.

It was like part of a dream to wander down the road in the evening and join the audience at a ceremony, watching the priest wring the neck of the sacrificial chicken and let the blood drip into a bowl; to take our chairs and go down another road some morning and watch the dancers performing a story from the Ramayana—the elaborate costumes, the men playing the gamelan, the incredible neck and arm movements of the child dancers whose perfection was a delight to the eye.

We would stop, one day or another, at the wood-carvers' village and watch the men making the intricately carved boxes and screens which we coveted—and some of which we bought. Or go to the village of the goldsmiths and see the men plying their beautiful craft—we still have the rings we purchased. Or we would stand motionless while women tied and dyed or, in the dimness of a shed, did their batik. Or we visited a temple, open to the sky, and saw the towering offerings of fruits and flowers carried on the heads of proud women, being laid at the altar. Or we were made welcome in a village where the women were weaving palm strips into intricate designs to decorate their offerings. And in one of them you motioned that you would like to try it, too . . . and did. The women clapped delightedly at your deftness, and one of them took the strip you had woven and put it gently around your hat. And in the evenings we listened to stories . . . the stories and legends of a people who civilization went back to ancient times and whose tales were dramatic and fanciful. We were all eyes and ears in those magical days. We knew, too, that sooner or later we would use what we had seen and heard.

Sumatra was a different experience, but definitely part of the whole. After that overnight trip in a small ship carrying pigs and copra and that undulated alarmingly to underground swells caused by a volcanic eruption, we were met at Padang by a handsome British Indian who was to be our guide and mentor. He took complete charge of us, removing tarantulas from our screened beds and releasing them on the verandah because, of course, he did not believe in destroying life; ordering our meals when we traveled across country and there would be no hotels; asking Father—who was always called the Mastah—not to let us sample the cookies that were so temptingly displayed by brilliantly dressed women at the local markets, and waiting for us to double up with cramps because Father would not so order us; picking a bouquet of gardenias for us with the dew still on them; introducing us to some of his Sikh friends at Medan and inveigling them to pose for you in our hotel room . . . . oh, Nanda was quite special and we often wondered what became of him, for he was a political rebel and a refugee from his native India.

We literally reeled across Sumatra, for the roads were one succession of curves—600, one day, in a comparatively few miles. We would wonder how Amsah, so small and with such slight wrists, could manage the big car, but he said, hitting his chest, "Amsah sterk!" (Amsah strong). And so he was. And we stood on the edge of Lake Toba, gazing down at the incredible blue, and wound through the forest with clouds of yellow butterflies fluttering in the sunlight and covering the hood of the car, and you said, "I'm going to paint his." The painting was bought by an interior decorator who did a whole room around it, and the painting you had done as a companion piece still hangs in our living-room. Whenever I look at it I am back in Sumatra . . . . with you.

Innumerable paintings grew out of that trip, and stories and articles. But they did out of all our trips, only this one had so much color and strangeness and beauty that perhaps it stands out above the others.

Lying in our mosquito rooms at night we could hear the tjichuks on the wall and we would talk over the day. We did that always, wherever we were—talking over the day's impressions with each other. It is one of the things I miss most sorely. Tippy would lie in his basket between our beds at home, and when the conversation went on too long, let out the most human sigh. It broke us up effectively. It was as if he said, "Oh, please lay off! I want to go to sleep."

So we would stop, laughing, and roll over and go to sleep, too, our minds full of the events we had been talking about, our hearts filled with gratitude for his companionship and this precious sharing.

I must still be grateful for the ineffable boon of having had it for so many years.

December

Dear,

There's a nip in the air, and snow is imminent, and Christmas decorations are up on the streets, and music greets one in every store, and starry-eyed children gaze in shop windows, and the holiday spirit is building up to its climax. And I shiver and wonder bleakly how I will make it through this first holiday season without you.

It was always such a happy time. My first Christmas tree—when I was four months old—was lit with candles, with Father standing by with a bucket of water in case anything happened. But after that it was decorated with Austrian lights in the shape of fruits and flowers and nuts.

After you came along it was only for a few years that we crept downstairs to find a gaily decorated tree waiting for us. As soon as we were able to join in, we decorated the tree on Christmas Eve, to help Santa Claus "because, you know, he had so much to do." And the Christmas Eve celebration became a part of our tradition.

Oddly enough, we never observed Sinterklaas in our household, which was rather strange, for Father had grown up with it, of course, and had told us about it every year. But the sixth of December in our household was like any other December day, and all our efforts were bent toward the 24th. The only resemblance to the Dutch observance of Sinterklaas was that Father would wrap some of our presents in box after box after box, and the bigger the first parcel was the more sure we were that the final one would be very small and contain something very special.

There was the time you undid a carton, and each of twenty-two boxes, all wrapped in newspapers and tissue paper and tied with string that had plenty of knots, and found, in the final, tiny box a little gold ring with a turquoise stone. Your ecstacy was a joy to see, for you had glimpsed the ring in a store window downtown and could talk of nothing else for days. And there was the time I opened paper bag after paper bag after paper bag to discover in the last one a gay verse promising me a trip to Cincinnati.

74

Those verses! Christmas was always a time for expending our utmost talent, if any, on verses describing the gifts or hinting at them or being mysterious about them, or humorous about them. After all the parcels and boxes had been opened, and the papers gathered up and the ribbons neatly folded and the rosettes laid away, we sat around the dining-room-table—for we had to have room to spread out all the papers—and we each took our turn reading the verses we had acquired. That is, we read them for the second time, because we had to read aloud whatever verse obtained to whatever package at the time we opened it. Now we had an opportunity to appreciate the wit and cleverness of the author, and perhaps that's what kept us at it for all those years, for we certainly did not spare our praise. You and Father had a particular aptitude for unusual meters and intriguing twists, and there for a while I was an ardent copier of Ogden Nash. They were easy to do and one could be as outrageous as one wished, knowing one would still not surpass Ogden himself. Even so, I think he would have been amused at some of the things that came from trying to imitate him.

After the verses, we gathered around the piano— or, in later years, the organ—and one parent or the other sat down and played Christmas music and we all sang together. Silent Night, of course, was our favorite, and somehow the tears always came with the singing . . . .

because the song itself was so lovely, and the organ sounded so full and rich, and we were together.

Then there was wine or hot chocolate and the cookies Anna had baked and little sandwiches . . . the tree lights blinking beautifully and the reflection of the lit tree illuminating the long windows, and Teddy or Tippy sharing the feast with crumbs specially given him. The ritual was always the same and yet, somehow, always different.

Santa Claus was not a complete mystery to us, for one year he came to the house while we were up. It was in Cincinnati, and it was the year when you were getting a bit dubious about Santa. "Do you really believe there is a Santa Claus?" you would ask me anxiously. You wanted to be reassured, and I out of sisterly concern and a magnanimous feeling of how wonderful it was to have superior knowledge, said, "Of course there is!" I knew better—but I hated knowing better. This gave me a chance to bolster up your tottering faith and to reassure myself a little bit, for I had to act as if I still believed, and that was pleasant. I hoped it would go on for years!

That, then, was the year that Santa came to the house. We were upstairs on the Eve, when the doorbell rang. Father was downstairs and answered it. "Mr. de-Leeuw?" asked a big booming voice that sent shivers through us.

"Yes," came Father's reassuring one.

"This is where Cateau and Adèle live, isn't it?" Santa Claus asked . . . for now we were sure this must be Santa Claus.

"It is," Father said. "Please come in, and can I get you something warm to drink?"

"No, thanks," Santa said, but we could tell he had come in. "Just my hands are cold, and I'll warm them at the fire. . . Tell me, Mr. deLeeuw, how have the girls been this year? Good, I hope?"

"Oh, very good," Father said, and you could have heard our sighs of relief downstairs. Perhaps, we thought, Santa did hear them.

"They've been quite extraordinarily good, in fact," Father went on. "They've helped their mother and done nice things for their grandmother, and their report cards have been excellent."

"No bad times at all?" Santa inquired genially. We suppose he had to ask a thing like that.

"Well," Father hesitated an appropriate moment, "there have been a few minor instances . . . like the time Adèle spoke rather sharply to her mother, and the time Cateau slammed the screen door when the cook particularly asked her not to—"

Santa interrupted. "Well, well, I know that children will be children, and the fact that you tell me they've been quite good otherwise is what I want to hear. Because I have these things with me, and I hope you'll lay them under the tree. I've got to be on my way—so much to do tonight, as you know. . . ."

We were nearly beside ourselves as we heard Father assure him that the presents would be properly placed and heard him ushering Santa out, and heard Santa's booming voice getting further away, and the front door closing. . . .

Mother, who had been surreptitiously holding on to your pinafore, let go now, and together we raced downstairs, breathless with excitement. "Where is he? Where is he? Did he have reindeers? Did he really have a beard and a red suit? Where are the presents?"

Father gave a magnificient wave of his hand and we tore into the living-room. Looking back I realize that Father seemed a little breathless himself, but it wasn't till years later that we confronted him with the idea that he was both Father and Santa Claus and I remembered his quizzical smile when he said, "Perhaps I should have been an actor. But anyhow it helped that I had a bass voice."

The other unforgettable experience was several years before that, when we both believed wholeheartedly and nothing could shake that belief. Aunt Betty had come to visit for the holidays, and on Christmas Eve, inexplicably, she said she had a bad headache and would have to go up to bed. We were terribly disappointed, for we wanted her to share in the festivities, but nothing could change her mind.

We were sitting, later, on the bottom step of the stairway, watching the colored flames in the hall fireplace, when there was a light knock at the door. At first we were not sure it was a knock, but then it came again, a little louder, and Mother answered. There, framed in the open doorway, with the porch light making diamonds of her crown, and the snowflakes falling, like back-drop scenery, stood the most beautiful vision we had ever seen. She had a silver wand with a glittering star on top, and her gown was blue net, with stars strewn over it and her long blonde hair fell on either side of her face to her shoulders. The Christmas Fairy herself! We recognized her at once, though we had only heard of such a creature, and never, never expected to have a visit from her.

She came slowly into the room and her voice, high and silvery, struck us with awe and delight. "I've come instead of Santa Claus," she said. She was real, she was real! Our mouths fell open. "Santa was busy and sent me, but he only sends me to homes where the children have been good all year, and this is your reward." She turned to Father. "Will you help me carry in the presents I have for Cateau and Adèle?" Father went out on the porch and came back with a silver sack that bulged delightfully. "I can't stay, you know," she said directly to us, "but I want you to have the happiest year ever, and to remember me." And with that she was gone, while we, unable to move, rubbed our eyes, wondering if we had dreamed the whole thing.

But the air was cold from the opened door, and the silver sack was being toted in to the Christmas tree. Aunt Betty! We must tell Aunt Betty what she had missed! It came to both of us at the same time and we started upstairs. Mother called, "Oh, first you must open at least one present, because Aunt Betty may still be resting."

So we tore the wrappings off two gifts and then rushed upstairs. "Aunt Betty! May we come in?" A muffled voice reached us, a sleepy voice. "Yes, dears. What is it?"

We told her, words tumbling over each other, of the miraculous vision. She gazed at us sympathetically, making reassuring noises as we burbled. The bedclothes were clutched up around her neck, her brown hair was spread out on the pillow. "But now do let me rest," she said, "and you can tell me all about it tomorrow. If I get to sleep again I think my headache will really be gone by morning."

We talked of it for days, and Aunt Betty must

have been heartily sick of hearing her costume and her acting described. For we believed in that visitation for years, and were the envy of our schoolmates. When we finally learned the truth we laughed with her over her madcap adventure. For she had had to run around the house—the back door was conveniently left open—climb the back stairs to her room, tear off her wig and throw it in a dresser drawer, toss her wand and crown in the closet—luckily we had been taught never to open anyone's closet—and get into bed, silver slippers and all, and pull the bedclothes up over her to cover the blue net gown before we got away from parental control and rushed to share the news with her. "Even if I nearly froze in that wispy gown, it was worth it to see your faces when I came in!" she said.

There were never quite those high spots again, but we kept the tradition of Christmas and its particular deLeeuw celebrations intact over the years. There was always a tree, of course, and there shall be one this year, my dear one. Johanna and I will decorate it, thinking constantly of you, in the way we had evolved for the past six years . . . all in gold, with golden balls large and small and golden tinsel and the golden butterflies and the little flower lights and the angel, in her gauzy dress and holding a light aloft, gracing the topmost branch.

We shall remember how, last year, you sat nearby in your crewel embroidered chair. That was the first time you were not able to take part in the actual tree-trimming. But with hands that shook with the Parkinson tremors you forced yourself to put the wires on the decorations and your voice was gay as you told us whether we should move things to right or left to get the desired effect. We talked then of other years when we invited friends to dinner and let them do the tree-trimming afterward—a brilliant idea, we thought, and I always ascribed to my executive ability, getting other people to do the work! Now Johanna and I must do it ourselves, for somehow I do not think I could see that gathering of friends when you were not among them.

Tom-Tom seems to think the occasion was invented just for him. He sniffs at the green branches (our watchful eyes make sure that he does no more than sniff!) and digs his inquisitive nose into the boxes and paws at the tissue papers lying about and chases an escaped golden ball all over the floor with delicate paws. He adores packages, as Tippy did, and when Christmas comes and he gets his own gaily wrapped boxes he will undo them with a wild-eyed frenzy, tearing at the ribbons with his teeth and strewing bits of paper over the rug and managing to get at the bone or yummies or playthings in one minute flat, and then panting up at us as if to say, "I got *that* open! What's next?"

How am I going to get through this season that

should be all joyous and warm and bright, with my heart dark and my mind blank and the tears so near the surface? I must remember . . . . remember . . . . no matter how it tears at me . . . . making the 'glug' and the bourbon balls and the fruit balls and the fudge and the nut cookies, decorating the little baskets, wrapping the sweets in foil and red paper, and carrying them to the friends we always chose to receive them. I must remember . . . and invite old friends, and new, to share the fruit cake and the wine and the songs around the piano. I must remember . . . and undo my gifts with love in my heart that I am remembered. I must do these things again this year, for you, and perhaps in that way I will be doing them for me. But as I write I do not know where I will get the strength to carry out my resolve.

January

Darling Toto,

Another year. A new year. Three hundred and sixty-five days to live through. How? One day at a time, I keep telling myself, as if I were an alcoholic. Take one day at a time, as I have been trying to do. Time heals all wounds, they say. I can't believe it. Yet I must believe it. Happy New Year! friends cry, coming in the door with armloads of flowers or a freshly baked cake. Happy New Year they call out, lifting their glasses. Happy New Year echoes madly in my brain. How can it be? They mean well, and I must smile and return the greeting. I mean it for them, I truly do, but how can they think it will be happy for me?

There's an ice storm today. It was late in coming.

For so many years it came on the first of January, usually just as we were getting ready to go to an Open House. I can see us, standing by the windows in the library, looking out at the glittering trees and the slippery street and the diamond-bright bushes, and hear us wondering aloud if we'd be foolish to try to go?

"Well, I'm willing if you are," you always said. "And at least," you'd go on with great satisfaction, "I started my new book today." That had become a kind of tradition, to begin a new novel on the first day of the year. This year I followed it, too, because in some strange way it made me feel close to you.

The minister's house was our first stop—usually there were three or four Open Houses that we had to visit. And the minister always said, as he opened the door to us, "Did you start it?" And you would say, "Of course," and he would shake his head and say, "I suppose it will be finished by March first?" "If not February 28th," you'd reply.

He was a delightful man, with a zest for life and a wonderful sense of humor and a philosophy that was so simple and all-embracing that it was deceiving. For he believed in love. "Love one another," he said, Sunday after Sunday. "Love the world. Love doing good. Love being alive." He believed that if people truly loved, there would be scant need for churches and Sunday service. It was too hard for people. They wanted a sermon on the situation in the Middle East or the migrant workers or the latest political scandal. They could sit back and ponder that and feel righteous. But to love? That was too simple . . . and much too difficult.

He's gone now. Where? I don't think we ever discussed that with him. But I rather think he would have agreed with the philosophy I put down on paper recently. I wish you could have seen it. Not that it would have been anything new to you—we believed so many things alike, we had the same outlook on issues so often. I like to think that you would have nodded in agreement as you read, and I can almost hear you saying, "Good for you . . . . well put."

I tried it out on our club—on two of our clubs, as a matter of fact. The reactions were decidedly interesting and not altogether what I had expected. In the first case— the all-female gathering—there was polite silence and attentive listening and finally, at one point, a protest! It was almost too much, obviously, for some of the more ortho- dox, that I could question a conventional, personal God's wisdom in making good people suffer and my rejection of the true believer's idea of Heaven. At the other gathering, the one made up of professional writers and artists, the reception was almost frightening in its intensity. You could literally have heard a pin drop. Afterward the members swarmed around me saying, "That's exactly what I think!" or "I'm so glad you put it into words—it's what I have believed but never formulated."

To put down one's philosophy is a salutary exercise and I'm glad I did it. (It also gave me the chance to do two papers for the mental exercise of one!) In it I put down quite rationally that it took true strength to live this life, accepting its sorrows as happenings and not as the cruel hand of One on High, that it was Nature who caused things to happen, without regard for the personal and the human, and that, by accepting, we proved our inner strength. Oh, it was easy to put into words! But to live that acceptance, I find, is the hardest thing I have ever done or shall be called upon to do. For I must accept your death as part of life and adjust to my loss, and this is my daily struggle.

Some people get comfort from thinking, and saying, "God is so good!" or "He has called him home." But I cannot stomach the thought of an Omnipotent One getting satisfaction from watching the suffering of someone like you, or our darling grandmother writhing in the agony of gangrene. This was Nature the uncaring, Nature the experimenter. One can accept Nature, but not a God who countenances babies held over gas flames and women beaten to death and men spilling their guts in war.

Even so, it is one thing to philosophize on paper,

and quite another to live that philosophy daily. Fortunately we were taught, early and late, to appreciate, to love, and to enjoy the wonder and the beauty of the world around us. This can be one's comfort, one's strength, and, perhaps, one's raison d'être.

I remember a sunny morning when we were at breakfast and you looked across at me and said calmly, "What will you do when I die?"

The tears welled up in my eyes. "I won't even think about it," I said.

"But you must. Would you go on living here?" you asked.

There was something compelling in your voice. You wanted an answer from me. I looked around, at the furniture we'd chosen, out at the garden that we had planted and was coming into bloom—it was a beautiful spring day—thought in rapid succession, like pictures flashing on a screen, of the things we had done together, the craft room, the row of books, the walks with the dogs, the tea parties for friends, the candle-lit dinners in this room . . . . and I said, above the lump in my throat, "I suppose so."

"I hope you will," you said, in that same calm voice that tore at me. "I would like to think that you would. We have been so happy here."

And I'm trying. Some people, I know, flee the

scene of the happiness they have shared with another. They get rid of mementos and appurtenances, they choose another house, another style of life. But I shall get my comfort from the dear and familiar . . . . from your paintings hanging on the walls, the chair you embroidered, the table mats you wove, the antique French blue glass plate set to catch the sun and that lays its color magic on Tom-Tom's ears as he basks on the rug. A thousand things that we chose together—like the crystal candlesticks we bought before we had any furniture!—and that we loved, like the leather bound books one of our publishers sent us every Christmas. The list can grow and grow . . . . the dear and familiar, the comfort upon comfort. How could one give up these reminders of shared happiness to start a new life with new things?

Each painting, for instance, brings up its own succession of scenes. The Spanish Girl, hanging over the couch, has from the beginning elicited the question, "Who posed for it—did you?" And I have my stock reply, "No, only for the hands and as a model to drape things on." But mentally I remember the sessions in your studio. "Sit straighter . . . . not that way, more relaxed, but not slouching." "Now I've got the mantilla just right on your head, so don't move." "Hold the fan slightly against your chest, as if you were just ready to use it." "Ah, you shifted your leg and the gold skirt has moved . . . wait, I'll fix it."

While you squinted at me and dabbed at your palette with a sure brush and brought the canvas to life with swift perfection we would talk of all kinds of things, we were never at a loss for things to talk about, and finally you would say, "Fifteen minutes! Get up and stretch." Those were good times, and privately I think you made me do more than was covered by the bounds of duty! The way you studied anatomy on me on the train commuting to New York—"Lean forward!" feeling along my backbone which was very prominent, glancing in your Gray's Anatomy, making me flex my arm while you located the deltoid, asking me to turn my head again while you commented on the many different ways ears were set along the jaw! What success you attained is partly due to me, I can think smugly.

Tom-Tom has been chasing a cellophane ball and it got under the credenza. His grunts and snufflings as he tries to get it out, rear up in the air, made me laugh. And suddenly I thought of how many things we used to laugh about . . . . laugh sometimes till we held our sides. Did I ever tell you that you had the most delightful laugh? It was so gay and infectious that others would laugh, too, without quite knowing what it was all about. The ability to enjoy a situation, to see the comic side, to appreciate a joke or a well-turned quip never left you, even when you were ill. That's one of the things that so many people remember about you—your gaity of spirit, and it is one of the things that I cherish most.

Tom-Tom has given up and come over to me, looking up with those beautiful hazel eyes and pleading, "Get it for me, won't you? I've tried everything."

So get it I must, I suppose . . . though I know very well that as soon as I do and he plays with it a few minutes it will land under the credenza again. I suppose that's love. Nothing is too much to do for the loved one. You could never do enough for Tippy—and me—and I would gladly have tried to carry the world on my shoulders if it would have helped you or pleased you . . . . or saved you.

Tippy. Every time I mention him or look at his photograph sitting on your desk I think of his story and how many times we told it to people. From repetition it got so that we could fill in a sentence for each other, but we never tired of telling it, and it seemed that people never got tired of hearing it because one friend told another. We always said we were going to write it as a story, a true story, and people would ask, "Have you done Tippy's story yet?" But somehow we never did, perhaps because it was too close at first, and then because there always seemed to be so many other things to do, deadlines to meet, contracts to honor, and we would say, "It can wait. In the waiting maybe we will refine it down to its essence."

Just the other day I had to tell it again, and that's what has brought it up now. If I told it to a group of friends, you would sit by, smiling, nodding your head, or putting in a word. And if you told it, I sat the same way . . . we loved the story as we loved Tippy.

When I was leaving for Holland that last time, and you were staying home, I asked you what you would like me to bring you, and you said, without hesitation, "One of the Countess's cairns." I took it lightly, for I saw no chance of doing it—it had been years since we had been traveling as a family together in Holland and had stopped to see the Countess van N van Z's famous kennel of cairns. Prize-winners all, beautiful grey or brindle or wheaten bundles of fur and energy. At the time we couldn't get one for we were traveling over Europe for some months. But we never forgot those adorable creatures and every cairn we saw was held up to our mental picture of their perfection.

Getting one of them for you was another matter. I really wondered if it would be possible, but I didn't want to sound too discouraging, since this was absolutely the only thing you wanted. How did I know if the Countess was still alive—if she was still breeding cairns—if she was still selling them? As it turned out my schedule abroad was hectic. Aunt Hetty, while I stayed in Scheveningen, had something planned for me every day, if not twice a day—

tea with her friends, lunch at a new restaurant (or an old one noted for its food!), a concert in the evening, an outing to a nearby lake, a ride in her open Packard, dinners with friends . . . . it went on and on, and every day she brought me a different kind of chocolate and watched me eat it so she could ask my opinion of it as compared to the previous one, and every day she corrected my Dutch pronunciation and then exhibited me proudly as an American (but with a Dutch father, my dear!) to her admiring acquaintances, and every day she came with the next day's schedule, so that it was just five days before I left that I found a moment to phone the Countess. I sighed with relief when she said yes, she still had cairns, but there was only one she would think of selling and that one was a year old. This put me back a bit; I had envisioned a small puppy, or a very young dog, as we had seen. The next hurdle was finding a date we could both meet, but finally that, too, was worked out and I went with Aunt Hetty to see 'the year-old male.'

After a little visit in the Countess' lovely drawing room with its Aubusson rugs and handsome bibelots we went out into the garden and she gave a low whistle. Around the building came two cairns—a grey one and a wheaten one, running side by side, their square feet barely touching the lush grass, their ears alert, their tongues hanging out. The Countess swooped down and took up the grey one, while the wheaten one, never pausing, ran on around the house. She cuddled him against her and said, "This is Tippy of Duinrell, the one I told you about," and he turned in her arms and gave my outstretched hand a little lick. I was his from that moment . . . but he was to be yours even more.

Then she told me his story. "I had sold him," she said, "to a family who were kind to him and who had children, but I think they were rather matter-of-fact— 'come here', 'do that,'—and Tippy is a dog who needs a great deal of loving. So he came back to the estate, and I kept him for a few days and then returned him to the family. A short while after he was back here again, and again I took him back. I thought, of course, he was honesick for us and for his kennel-mates. This happened four times, and four times I returned him, but then I knew it could not go on, he was not happy there, so I kept him as one of my house-dogs and gave them another cairn—who seems perfectly content there. That is why," she said, looking at me searchingly "that I will not part with him again unless I am sure he will get a great deal of attention and loving. Are you sure he will?" I could answer without hesitation, "Absolutely sure. He will be adored."

We made the necessary arrangements for sending

him—because it was too late to get his inoculations for entry before I left. When I came back to New York and you and Mother met me and I told you what I had done, you were thrilled. It was several weeks before we got the cable announcing that Tippy was being shipped by air. We went to the airport—it was a hot muggy day—and began our five-hour wait for him. We had brought newspapers, in case he might be ill, and a bottle of water, which was getting warmer and warmer, and a little dish so we could give him some food, and we saved part of our chicken sandwiches to feed him.

After those five hours he was brought in a handsome wooden Quonset-type carrier and set on the counter. His leash came through a little grill in the front and was attached to a nail in the round roof, and printed over the doorway was "Valuable dog." Behind the grill we could glimpse a bit of grey fur, and you stuck your finger through and his black muzzle was pressed against the grating and his pink tongue curled around your finger. While I signed papers you took him out, running pell-mell down the concrete steps, to the grassy stretch in front of the building. Around and around you went, with him stopping eagerly at every bush and every fire hydrant. When I finally got out, we offered him the warm water—which he disdained—and a piece of chicken, which he did not want, and we got in the car, the Quonset carrier stored in the trunk, and started home.

Tippy hopped up on the back ledge and sat there, with me beside him, newspapers spread over my lap—in case. You kept looking in the rear-view mirror. "His one ear is down," you said, and yes, it was. "But never mind, I don't care!" you hastened to say. "I think he's perfect, absolutely perfect!" When he eventually hopped down to snuggle against me his ear was up, and we both laughed, realizing that it had been bent by the slope of the car and was not a defect!

Before he came you had Mr. A., our dear old carpenter, rebuild the dog-house Father had made for Teddy. It had been newly painted and with a new roof, and a new piece of carpeting leading from the angled doorway into the house itself. The windows had been painted to look as if they had Dutch shutters, and above the door you had painted, "Awas Antjing!" Beware of the dog. Beware of the dog indeed! When we tried to lure Tippy into it he would not budge. He looked up as if to say, "Somebody got me into the cage-thing for the trip, but now I'm wise, and I'll never enter one again." And he never did!

You let all your writing go while you got acquainted with your new treasure, taking him for walks around the property and down the street, sitting with him beside you, feeding him, loving him. When his papers came, we chuckled over the combination of names in his ancestry, wondering, for the hundredth time, who thinks up these fancy monikers. But when we saw the address of his former owners we were puzzled. Where in Holland was Oisterwijk? We had never heard of it.

We got out maps of Holland, hunted over and over again, in an ever-widening circle near Wassenaar where the Countess lived. Finally we gave up and wrote to Aunt Hetty. "Is there such a place as Oisterwijk?" we demanded, and she air mailed back, "Of course. It is on the other side of Holland, Near Tilburg." We stared at one another in amazement. Near Tilburg . . . ninety miles, 150 kilometers away from his former home! Before he was a year old he had made that trip four times. It was, literally, another 'Incredible Journey.' But to be back at the home he had loved and with the people he had loved he had walked that distance four times, cadging food, catching mice, perhaps, in the fields, crossing bridges, or swimming brooks, sleeping wherever he could find shelter for the night. He must have been terribly unkempt and soiled and weary when he came back to the estate. No wonder the Countess had said she would not sell him again unless she knew he would be properly loved!

Love he never lacked. He slept between our

beds, he went with you to your studio every day, he curled up on the rug at your feet while you read or needle-pointed in the evening, he ran madly from one end of the house to the other whenever you returned after being away for an hour. And when you put him on your shoulder he clung so hard that you did not even need to put your hand on him to hold him there. "You could not have given me anything I treasured more," you told me time and again. "He's the best present I ever had." And I would think how narrowly I had missed getting him for you. Fourteen years! How incredibly swiftly they passed, but how rich they were with your mutual love and devotion! When we walked him your pride was a visible thing, and when children stopped to stroke him and asked, "Is it a boy dog or a girl dog?," your laugh would ring out. "I know it's hard to tell," you would say, "but he *is* a boy dog."

When you took him to obedience school the instructor took one look and said, "This dog has been shown," and so he had—he had won a first in the puppy class at Amsterdam. He was the only male in a class of ten, which made it difficult sometimes for him to concentrate on the lesson, but when he graduated he was third. "He would have had a first," the judge said sternly to you, "if you had not been impatient." But you were so eager for him to show off that you had repeated a command. He proved that evening what a complete ham he was. When the audience applauded he positively smirked before he sat down beside you. And then, after Number Two went through its paces and everyone applauded, Tippy got up, faced the audience, and bowed and smirked again. It was for him, of course, he obviously thought. This happened eight more times, and by then the audience was hysterical. We, too, were laughing so hard that we had difficulty carrying off his mortar board, his can of dog food, his little 'gold cup,' and his new leash!

The actor in him had plenty of occasions to come to the fore. When we took him with us to Hamilton, where we were to do a round of speaking and autographing, we found that a frenzied schedule had been arranged for us—but also, that we had been given a delightful house for our stay and young girls to act as dog-sitters for our evenings out. Tippy made friends of them all, and during the day we decided, whenever possible, to take him with us to the Library where we spoke and to school assemblies. At the schools we generally had first to visit the elementary classes for which there was not room in the auditorium, and neither of us ever forgot the picture of the children rushing forward, as we entered the room, and squatting down and patting his grey head and his grey rump. One could hardly see dog for the mass of patting hands. He would stand perfectly still while they petted him, tongue out, tail wagging. He was always marvelous with children, and they loved him on sight.

It was when we spoke on stage that he decided to hog the scene. After I spoke there was applause—but Tippy went forward to the footlights to take it unto himself. And when you spoke he sat quietly beside me until the applause came, and then he darted forward and grinned from side to side, absolutely certain that the clapping was just for him. It wowed the children, and all the letters that they wrote after we returned home referred to him in one way or another. One of the letters we cherished most said candidly, "The authors weren't as old as we thought they would be, but it was their dog Tippy that was the most fun."

He had infinite charisma, all right. People who had seen him only once or twice remembered him in their phone calls or letters. Children who were deeply afraid of dogs could not resist his appeal and came closer to pat him—and later to own a dog themselves. That made you very proud. As he grew older he grew even sweeter, with a devotion that was touching, and when he was finally ill his nobility in suffering was incredible, and when he died and was buried under the dogwood and near the bed of tu-lips—because, after all, he was a Dutch dog—a part of your heart was buried with him.

February

Dear Valentine,

I'm writing this on the day given over to the saint himself because we always made so much of it. For that matter, we made a good deal of any special day in the year and I like to think that it meant we felt life's special occasions were worth celebrating. I still feel so, only now I am celebrating merely in memory. Perhaps next year——

The florist's delivery just came to the door with a huge paper-wrapped cone of flowers and a potted plant, and when I saw them I was overcome with grief. I remembered with a rush all the times I had sent you flowers and you had sent them to me on this day. Apparently it was our childish conceit that neither of us would know from whom they came—there was never a card, of course, or any outward indication that they could not have been from some admirer or friend. Yet why wouldn't I know that the extravagant bouquet of freesia was from you—you who knew of my particular love for those delicious flowers and in tribute to the poem I had written about them years ago? And why should I think you wouldn't recognize who had sent your favorite yellow roses and mignonette because only I knew that your favorite painting was of roses and mignonette from our garden at the Big House? These were secrets we shared, blithely ignoring the fact that they were not secrets to each other.

It was fun to have a tea, with all the appropriate decorations, for our friends: little red hearts on the cupcakes, red hearts on the sugar lumps, red roses in the centerpiece, and heart-shaped baskets of candy. Then one year you went even further and drew an enormous red heart out of drawing paper. Across it you printed, "We love you!" and hung it on the outside of the door to greet our friends. What laughs we had when the postman took it to himself and the delivery man asked whom it was for and some children, who had come to sell subscriptions, chirped, "We love you, too . . . But who are you?"

I still have the big red heart, and next year I shall hang it out again for anyone, and everyone, to see. I keep saying that to myself, "Next year . . . next year." Will I be able to do all these things that I have promised myself? Will I be strong enough? Will doing them break me down or give me a strength I lack now and so urgently need?

February needs a day of this kind, for it is a bitter month. The snow lies deep against the windows; there is no place for poor Tom-Tom to go outside until the gardeners come to shovel out his patio. The trees are bowed with the weight of snow, and all traffic is muted—and meager—down our lane. People are at home with colds or the flu, doctors are harrassed, phones are out of order, deliveries are erratic and I momentarily expect the furnace to quit, although it has functioned perfectly for months on end. It is a month simply to live through as best one can, hoping that March, whatever its reputation, will somehow be better. At least, one tells oneself, it can hardly be worse.

But February has a warm spot in my mind, in spite of everything, because that is the month when we usually set out for foreign parts. How many years on end did all fall and early winter plans mature into a trip abroad? It was a good time to get away and a particularly good time to go back to Holland. For in Holland the flowers would be blooming—incredible as it always seemed—and pushcarts of luscious vegetables would be wheeled through the streets and the air would have a springlike feel to it, even as the winds from the North Sea made us shiver in our woollies.

To watch spring slowly, steadily, creep into the countryside was a yearly delight, a never-failing one. In Holland spring was really spring, a gradual, inevitable unfolding of bud and leaf, of green shoots pushing up through the earth, of fragrance everywhere.

I'm constantly tempted to say, "Do you remember—?" Do you remember (oh, how futile of me to say this; it is *I* who must remember) the first time we left for Holland? It was a miserable winter day with the driveway so deep in snow that we had to wait for men to come to clear it, and then the brakes caught fire on our way to the dock, and we barely made it up the gangplank? But once aboard, the ship life took over and we were cozzened and petted and treated so royally that we hated to get off eight days later. The dock at Rotterdam was lined with shouting, waving, talking, animated Hollanders looking for their relatives and friends, and we turned to each other and said in surprise, "Who ever said the Dutch were stolid?"

It was to be borne in on us time and time again how wrongly the Hollanders have been classified in other people's minds. They're not all blond or heavyweights or stolid or Protestant—they're dark and thin and volatile and animated and Catholic, too. We knew that, of course, from reading it and hearing it from Father, but seeing Hollanders en masse for the first time came with the shock of a revelation. I can still recall Father's amused smile when we turned to him and exclaimed over our discovery.

If we as Americans had misconceptions, Hollanders had them, too, about us. How many times did we explain that not everyone was rich, that there were gangsters, yes, in Chicago, but not everyone was a gangster, that we knew Bach and Goethe and other European greats, and that Roosevelt was not necessarily going to save the world? It was gratifying, though, to have them compliment us extravagantly on our stumbling Dutch . . . it was impossible to say more than a few brief sentences in Dutch because they were so eager to practice their English . . . and their spontaneous and endless kindnesses were a joy every day. A street urchin offering to show us the way, an elderly woman proffering her umbrella when we were caught in a shower, a man helping us onto a streetcar with our packages, a woman, when we were on a tour of hofjes, bidding us come in and have a cup of tea . . . in return for which Father sat down at her little parlor organ and played for her, in return for which she offered us our choice of a litter of kittens!

I think it was typical of Holland that it did not strike us 'all of a heap,' as some countries do, but crept into our hearts in the same slow, insistent, pervasive way that spring crept over the countryside that first visit. It opened its heart to us as we opened our hearts to it, and with each subsequent visit we grew to know and love it better.

There's never anything quite like a first experience. Every impression, every incident, is so fresh and vivid. The sights, the smells, the tastes strike one with the impact of discovery. I always hoped I had some of that freshness when I called my book The Flavor Holland—the first time, for instance, that you see the acres upon acres of hyacinths and tulips and daffodils, the first time you see the grass-grown walls of ancient towns, the first time you taste Dover sole and baby carrots and the Dutch version of pea soup. The food, of course, was one delight after another— white asparagus as large around as your thumb, drowned in butter, the currant buns, the tender veal, the cookies distinctive of every community.

It was so good to get to know Father's country under his guidance. History came alive as he told it—the battle of the Sea Beggars, the death of William of Orange, the frightful siege of Leyden, the lives of the staunch brothers deWitt, the building of the dikes. . . . The only time I remember Father getting a bit wrothy was when I came home from school with the tale of the boy putting his finger in the dike to hold back the water! All the stories were part of the building of the country and a stirring history it is. We were proud to have it in our background, and each place we visited in our leisurely fashion had a distinct flavor of its own because of his stories.

We were proud, too, when Hollanders told Father he spoke such a beautiful Dutch. They were both admiring and incredulous, for the average Hollanders had grown careless of endings and had a peculiar gutteral quality that Father's voice and intonation lacked. "Perhaps it's because I've been away so long," he said mildly. At any rate they would often ask him to say something over again, just for the pleasure of hearing it 'as it used to be,' they would sigh.

Markets and old towns and churches and castles . . . we saw them all, as we moved in quiet fashion from one place to another, spending a week here, a few days there, a month elsewhere. I was given charge of making hotel reservations, I recall, and while we were in Rotterdam I wrote to a small, private hotel in Haarlem, stating our requirements and ending, "If you can furnish these accommodations, please wire collect." In a few hours a telegram was delivered to our rooms. "Collect," it said. It caused the family endless amusement, but, as I said, it was obvious that we did have the requested accommodations!

No matter how much we did and saw there was

always something left to be experienced, and we would take comfort in the fact—it was more than a hope—that there would be a next time. Meanwhile, I was taking notes madly and you were painting equally madly. Your experiences, however, were more varied and exciting than mine. When you had a studio in Volendam, across the street from the hotel, one of your models proved to be a young man who was mad. When you painted in the Mauritshuis you had only a week to complete a Vermeer copy, and had to run around from our hotel to the gallery, each day, set up your easel, paint for an hour, and take it down again. When you set up your equipment in the marketplace at Middelburg, the crowd that gathered to watch you effectively obliterated the scene you were trying to paint, and when you would ask them to move they would reluctantly do so for a minute or two and then come back again. And on one of our visits, when our hotel caught fire and we were evacuated, the pastry cook, who had watched you painting in the hotel garden while he rolled out pie dough in the basement, risked his life to go up to our rooms and bring down your paintings!

That reminds me that it was also in this miserable month of February that you started the Art Association here. At twenty-one it was a brash and reckless thing to attempt—as everyone told you, no one more articulately than Miss W., the history teacher who had to be taught how to say your name. She was very positive. "It has been tried in this town several times," she told you earnestly, "and never succeeded. Why do you think you could do what older, more experienced people have failed to do?" "I don't know," you replied, "except that I want to try it. I can't succeed, can I, unless I try?"

If we as a family had any doubts about your ability to swing it, we wisely kept them to ourselves. You wrote out two hundred invitations to a first meeting. "Where would we put two hundred people?" I inquired. "If twenty come I'll be happy," you said. And fifty came. You gave a warm, succinct, enthusiastic talk, and all fifty signed up as charter members and elected you president. With an uncanny instinct you appointed the slightly eccentric scion of a well-known family as the membership chairman, and she, entranced with her mission, rode all over town on her bicycle, inveigling friends and acquaintances to join the group. In less than five months she had signed up two hundred and fifty members.

It went on from there. We got the use of the Library art gallery and every month there was a program on one of the arts—dancing, sculpture, painting with demonstrations, music, poetry and pottery. It was the talk of the town.

Those were busy, exciting times . . . and great

fun as well, in spite of occasional headaches. But if sometimes a speaker failed to turn up, someone else was always
found in time, and on Art Association nights the broad
stairs to the upper floor echoed to tramping feet. There
were hostesses to get for exhibition hours, there were
hostesses to tie up for the opening teas and Sunday after-
noons, there were dancers or puppeteers to fetch from the
railroad station. But it all worked out, and the gratifying
thing to both of us, but of course to you especially, was the
willingness of people to take part in this new venture and
even to attach a certain éclat to being asked.

One of the highlights of the association, and an
absolutely ridiculous thing to undertake, was the English
Village, complete with scenery, booths where artisans
worked, appropriate music, and costumed salespeople. It
couldn't be done . . . but it was, and years afterward
people were still talking about it. "We must have another!"
they cried—those who hadn't had any thing to do with it, of
course. But those who had worked themselves to the bone
and stayed up all night into the morning said, "Once was
enough!" Just the same, it was a real landmark, and no one
was more commendatory than Miss W., who had said the
association itself was impossible.

I still serve little sandwiches on the silver tray the
grateful directors gave you on the twenty-fifth anniversary
of your 'baby,' and on the wall of your studio is the

medallion with its gay red ribbon in acknowledgment of your presidency.

And then it happened, as it has happend to so many organizations that are started with faith and hard work and become prosperous . . . other people wanted to be in power and did not know how to use it; money was saved by the frugal and spent by the profligate; dissensions arose among officers. And finally the Art Association fell apart. But it lasted for fifty years, and of that you could be very proud.

I got out a packet of the program announcement cards that we had saved, and conjured up some of the performers in my mind's eye. But mostly I saw you—you standing in front of the audience handling the business meeting with dispatch so that we could get to the entertainment, or donning a smock and doing a quick sketch, or moving about the gallery in a long dress and flowers at your shoulder, the gracious hostess at an opening night. I see you, your beautiful eyes sparkling, your quick smile that nevertheless lingered, I hear your voice, so feminine and clear, and the laughs that would run through the audience at your spontaneous wit . . . and I close my eyes to keep the scene intact for a while. You gave so much of yourself to others, you gave so unutterably much to me. I can never be grateful enough.

March

Toto, dear,

Whenever I call you that, I think of Father, whose pet name for you it was. Of course we were both Bunny or Chickie, but Toto was entirely yours, as Dédé was mine.

There was such complete rapport between you and Father. You had something of his build, in a way, and his kind of hand and his quiet strength. I remember how you rode on his chest as a small child, delighting in rising and falling with his breathing, and how you played horse and camel and elephant on his accommodating feet, and how he managed to smile even when you pulled out his hair in an excess of happiness. Of course he had hair to spare, but it must have been somewhat uncomfortable!

You liked so many of the same things . . . thunderstorms and high seas and milk and honey and mystery stories and science. You had the same kind of mind—searching, keen, and analytical. Research was your special joy, and you got that, I know, from Father, for whom no problem was unsolvable as long as there was somewhere else to look or someone else to interview or something else to ponder. You both liked chess—while I got impatient if anyone took more than half a minute to think out the next move—and working in wood, and astronomy, and open fires, and rare steak. You were both self-sufficient—you often said you were a hermit at heart—but the focus of attention at a party, and neither of you liked the telephone and would go to great lengths to avoid making a call or even answering it.

I can chuckle now (thank God) over my mental picture of the two of us in the living-room, you reading, me with my lap full of assorted papers, going over a manuscript. The phone would ring, and neither of us would move. "The phone's ringing," you would say finally. "Yes, I know," I'd say, "would you mind answering it?" "Oh, you know how I hate talking on the phone!" you'd say plaintively. "You do it." "Can't you see I can hardly get up with all this stuff on my lap?" I'd inquire a bit testily. "I know, but do do it this time, won't you?" you'd answer with a wicked little smile. And so, the phone still ringing, I'd dump the papers on the floor and get up and answer. It happened over and over and I never won.

But when Mother was ill and dying, and the phone rang in the middle of the night, it was you who got up and took the receiver, and it was you who broke the news to me.

I don't think you ever, willingly, put in a call. You would go to see someone, or write a letter, rather than phone. "I'd never have a phone in the house if it were up to me," you would say firmly. "I don't see how you stand it, particularly when you're working." But I was always hopeful, I suppose, that it would be an editor panting for a new book or asking me to do a special article, or some friend inviting us to a party. Even when it turned out to be an insurance agent or somebody asking us to put out old clothes for a cerebal palsy drive I was not discouraged. If we planned a dinner ourselves, you were all eagerness— "but you do the phoning," you would invariably say. And if by chance you were passing the phone when it rang and there was no way out, you would pick it up, looking martyrlike, and almost immediately call out to me, "Do take this, Adèle. I can't hear a word, there's so much noise." You who had such acute ears that you could hear a pin drop on the third floor, were rendered helpless—so you inferred—by someone talking or a dog barking down the street or a vacuum going. It was your one eccentricity, and I loved you for it.

The wind is blowing a little gale today and the sky is steel grey. Something is brewing, and it is a good day to stay indoors. Even Tom-Tom thinks so and, though it is three-thirty and his usual walk-time, he is curled under my desk and is making no overtures, for which I am duly grateful. Yet the pussy willows are out and waving in the wind and the snowdrops have long since gone and the scilla are putting forth green shoots and the tulips are sending up spears of green. Spring can be just around the corner, as they say. Easter will be early this year, too, and I wonder how I will feel.

It would be comforting, I suppose, to believe in resurrection and the life everlasting, but I cannot. Neither of us could. It is much more comforting to me to celebrate the day as a paean to spring and the emergence of life again after the winter's blight. Yet, people would say, if you can celebrate that, why can you not believe it possible for human beings, too, to come into a new life? And this is beyond me. I think both of us felt the same way . . . that it was important to live the life we knew to the fullest, enjoying each day, each moment, making the most of our talents and our good fortune, rather than to look to some

improbable future where we would be rewarded and cozzened.

I miss talking about this sort of thing. You and I
were always able to discuss subjects, speculating, arguing,
agreeing. It was stimulating and good mental exercise.

"I have no fear of dying," you said more than
once. "I think oblivion would be a boon and a blessing."
Somehow, I could never go that far. I was the one who
wanted to live—well, perhaps not forever—but long
enough to see what the world would be like years and years
from now. Oblivion would be too final a solution to the
business of living. But you, who had battled pain for many
years of your life, saw it as a release.

"You can't leave me," I commanded. I shall never
forget your gentle smile when I talked like that.

"Someday I must," you said, in a voice that went
straight to my heart. "I wish you could adjust to that. You
are the one who will live on . . . but I will stay with you as
long as I can, that I promise."

It's queer how we can turn our minds from a
subject that distresses us. I turned away time and again
. . . and now I am really faced with living on—without you.

There was a phone call just now—another friend
off on a cruise. I wished her well, and began remembering
the sole cruise we went on, so long ago. Father couldn't go,

so Mother, you and I set sail for the Mediterranean. It was a leisurely one, eighty-odd days (some of them very odd!) ending up with a week in Paris on our own. Much as we enjoyed the exploration in different ports, from Gilbralter to Turkey, we got our chief pleasure from the conglomeration of people on board.

There was the hostess, a southern woman of indeterminate age, who was very, *very* southern, and who paraded around the decks dispensing smiles, four times a day, each time in a different costume. There was the young woman, pretty enough, but so rouged that you called her the Japanese Sunset. There was the man who said his sister had sent him on the cruise to find a wife and who attached himself to me. His dinner clothes were impeccable, and he boasted about his estate on the river, but his hair was frowsy, as if he'd just been out in a strong wind, and he couldn't dance. Being at an age when dancing was very important and enjoyable, I suffered agonies on the floor and was forever trying to think up a new excuse. When he asked you you sweetly said you had something the matter with your foot (which miraculously got better when a preferred partner came around) or you were resting or were about to go to the cabin. But that didn't have to happen often, you were always being whirled away by somebody or other. However, Mr. G., started up on me as soon as the dance music struck up, and my inventiveness got plenty of usage before the voyage was over.

There was the night of the talent show and you were scheduled to do a Spanish dance in costume, and the ship heaved and rolled and bucked so that all the little gold chairs slid from one end of the ballroom to the other and your dance became a real improvisation—a feat which made you known throughout the ship.

There was the fourteen-year old, precocious son of wealthy parents who attached himself to us, insisting on speaking only a kind of Jabberwocky he had made up (and which we understood) and who perched on our steamer chairs, telling us outrageous and very funny stories, and who loved to tease us by bringing the whole tray of tea cakes over to us, and telling decrepit old gentlemen that we were yearning to meet them and to do a waltz together.

There was the big, bony blonde who said right away that her trunk hadn't made it to the dock, and who wore the same drab brown outfit for the entire trip until everyone avoided her.

There was the wealthy Newport woman who swam in the pool dressed in a black silk suit with embroidered white nainsook collar and cuffs, her swanlike neck far out of the water, her perfect breast stroke measured and faultless.

There were endless characters aboard, which was entertainment enough, and my notebook and your sketch pad grew daily. But when we came to a port we saw human nature at its worst . . . and occasionally best, but very occasionally. One would have thought there would be no carriages or automobiles unless one stood first at the gangplank and shoved everyone else aside in a mad scramble to have a choice of vehicles drawn up alongside the dock. The fact that there were plenty at each port made no difference; the same mad scramble took place every time, and by the same people. Perhaps it was their way of getting some additional excitement. We learned soon enough to wait till everyone else had gone down and then we descended in a leisurely fashion, at which point, almost invariably, the guide or tour conductor or whoever was in charge, would wink, motion to a hidden vehicle around the corner, and off we went in style.

"Sometimes," you said wistfully, "it's hard to like the human race."

The memory of that voyage is a collage of scenes and experiences from the monkeys scampering along the corridors of the Gibralter fortress to the day we spent exploring the souks in Constantinople, coming upon an old friend living in the city and who took us home with her. It became a night to remember, for she called in half a dozen White Russian refugees who were her friends and we all made music together, and told stories, and you and a prince drew each other's portraits, and they all accompanied us down to the ship at sailing time. How often we lived over that evening and wondered what became of those men, so poor, so homeless, and yet so gallant?

We always loved life on shipboard, but this particular voyage had an added attraction. Father had letters waiting for us—served on a silver salver twice a week by our steward or the purser—and your current beau did likewise for you! (I still think he got the idea from Father!) We expected that kind of thing from Father, but you were very touched at the devotion—and the time he had to spend on composing—of your friend P. He was determined, obviously, not to let you forget him during those eighty days, and it worked.

When we went to South America later he did the same thing, only this time there were not only letters but flowers. The purser insisted on delivering those himself, and when you asked him how fresh flowers could be delivered on such a long trip he said he had instructions to buy them in port and keep them in the refrigerator until each appointed day. Unfortunately he then got the idea from P., and began sending you flowers himself, even managing a large bunch of forget-me-nots as far as Buenos Aires!

That was an unforgettable voyage, too . . . seas

smooth as silk, a first officer who taught us magic tricks, being asked daily to throw the dice for the horse races, and dancing every night.

Shaking dice for the horse races on deck became something of a problem. The first, second and third times were fun, but then we realized that some other women, or girls, on board, were looking at us rather icily. We decided to forego the event and kept to our cabins when the horse racing was to begin. "Aha," we thought after ten minutes or so, "this is working." Not so. Came the quarter hour and there was a knock at the door. The steward said respectfully, "You're wanted up on deck, miss—" nodding to both of us. We said hastily that we had laundry to do, or some such excuse, and he left. Next day we hid again, and again the steward came with the message. This time we were writing. He shook his head, as if to indicate that it was a palpable lie and no good would come of it. The next day when the knock came we had thought up another excuse, but the steward said firmly, "The captain said he wishes you to come up on deck."

There was no gainsaying the captain—when he asked you to do something, you did it. We went up, and there stood everything ready—the stewards with the horses lined up, people with their note books and change. "Well," said the captain, "we thought you were never coming. As we're half an hour late, we'll just keep the game going for an extra half hour." After that, we gave up. "But why did *we* have to do it?" we asked him later. "There were plenty of other women willing and eager." "Because people said you brought them luck," he said.

And we *were* lucky, weren't we? Lucky, not just with a game like horse racing (we never bet, of course, since we were shaking the dice), but in so many ways of life . . . in our parents, and our trips, and our dogs, and our home life. And above all, in each other.

The captain, a genial, elderly man, who always had to have his post-prandial promenade around the deck twice with one of us on each arm, would look with a kind of fatherly amusement at his radio officer who came down from his radio shack only to dance a waltz with me, disappearing immediately thereafter, and at you being whirled madly around the deck by an over-enthusiastic South American in a furious maxixe. He always said he was proud of you that you survived being tossed in the air at the conclusion without looking ruffled or breathless. As a matter of fact, you danced off ten pounds on that trip and I danced on ten . . . which did us both good.

We hated to leave Rio. It was an incredible place, with its curving shoreline bordered by the mosaic black and white walk that made one dizzy, the stunning Sugar

Loaf in the harbor, the hotel with its lace-trimmed linen sheets and elegant women, down from the fincas, with their fur capes and golden toothpicks. And of course Copacabana, where we gambled away two dollars and came out with four times that! At least it made a good article later on. It was only at intervals, and with quick side glances, that one saw the poverty rampant behind the facade of wealth, fantastic wealth. The other side of the golden coin was not pleasant.

When we trans-shipped, after that stay in Rio, for Buenos Aires, we were hailed by some Scottish men leaning over the rail (their ship had just come in from Spain), and we no sooner came on board than we were asked to dance. It seems they were tired of struggling with the Spanish language and some rather buxom females, so we had a rousing welcome. Next day one of the men asked you what number he should play in the ship's pool. You hadn't the vaguest idea but you said promptly, "Three." It turned out that the ship's mileage ended in a three, and there was jubilation and champagne. The next day you were asked again, and came up, quite as promptly, with eight. Eight it was . . . More champagne. The third day you suggested six, and it proved to be right. You were treated like a seeress, and nothing was too good for you. Half-seriously and half in jest they said they would like to use you in their business, but Father put his foot down on that! As for you, you said you were glad the trip only took three days to B. A., or you might have lost your seeress reputation.

We had looked forward to Buenos Aires and we were not disappointed. You were going to exercise your Castillian Spanish (the only one in your class who took it), but you practically never got a chance to use it. We were met at the dock by a tall, handsome young man who had been 'put at our service.' He had the figure of an athlete, and in fact was one of the city's most vaunted ones. At our service he was indeed. He presented himself at the hotel in the morning, took us to the shops, to nearby estates, to the beautiful club house bordering the race course—another chance to bet—and to the theatre and the opera. He brought mother extravagant bunches of flowers, violets especially, which he was astute enough to have discovered were her favorite flowers, and asked permission to take her daughters for a ride. The carriage would be waiting, and when we got in—I acted as a kind of duenna, I'm sure, for it was you he was interested in—he would get out his handkerchief and wipe our shoes, so that we need not have any of the common dust on our 'beautiful shoes.' He bought us tango records—we still have them—and pastries and chocolates, and lent a delightful air of romance to our stay. It didn't occur to us until later to wonder how Mother and Father spent the time when we were out exploring Buenos Aires with L.!

I suppose all travel is rewarding to the degree of your anticipation and your participation. In that we were lucky, too, for we loved traveling, and traveling together, we were ready for any small adventure that came our way, we enjoyed different people and different life styles. We liked as much luxury as we could afford, but we were game to rough it on those occasions when it was necessary. After all, a certain amount of discomfort lends itself to some marvelous stories when you get home.

Our travels found their way into books and articles and stories. And now they can be the basis of my memories. This is a major blessing, for in all of them you are there.

April

My dearest dear,

I've been going over your paintings and drawings—those that are left—and trying to decide what to do with them. There are those on the walls which I will never part with, and there are some others that I cannot bring myself to part with, either. But I think I have found a partial solution, and it came about because M. and A. were getting married.

What to give for a wedding gift? They were both working madly in their recently rented apartment, painting walls and woodwork, and A. said, "The walls are going to be so empty!" That's when it came to me, and I asked them to come to tea and choose one of your paintings as my—our—gift to them.

It really touched my heart to see their gratitude. And I stood by, while they agonized over a choice, mentally picking the one I hoped they would pick, and saying nothing that might influence them. Imagine my unbounded joy when they chose the one I wanted them to—the lovely, soft-toned nude with her back to the viewer and the rose drapery falling off the stool . . . the one an art critic had compared to Ingre. I was so pleased, and they were so proud that now I know where, eventually, other paintings will go—to people who loved your work and who are needing something for their walls. It will be good to know that they will have happy homes and be a constant joy to their owners.

When I stop to think about it, as now, I realize with something of a start how many of our friends and acquaintances are artists and writers. We always prided ourselves on our catholic tastes; we liked all kinds of people, in all kinds of fields, we took a wicked joy in putting different people together at dinner parties and seeing how the amalgam worked out. But looking over our friends I see how after all we seem to have gravitated to those who were in our own profession. And I suppose that is only natural. These are people with whom we could talk, or argue, or discuss, in whose achievements we could glory, who would understand our little triumphs and frustrations, and who, above all, were creative.

That's why we loved Listen-to-me so much. The name alone intrigued us—it had a wonderfully egotistical sound!—and when we were asked to join we went to the first meeting with real curiosity. It was such a happy congregation of professionals! Many of them are gone now, but I see them, each of them, with clear vision and remembrance. Some had wit, some true humor, some astounding cleverness with words, all of them had an inventiveness that gloried in the monthly assignments—a song for a troubadour, a speech in the style of Thomas Jefferson, a vignette on apples, a short short based on a given sentence . . . whatever it was, we all fell to and came up with some delicious results. The minutes alone were worth listening to, and secretaries, far from refusing the job, took it on with eagerness, if only to prove to the members that they could be even cleverer than the previous holder of the position. We wrote fables and one-act plays and articles and poems and scripts, there was a minimum of business, and, best of all, no one could hold forth longer than his allotted fifteen or twenty minutes.

How could I ever forget Edgar Stehli on a high ladder, trimming an imaginary Christmas tree while the audience held its collective breath for fear he would fall? Or Henry Hall pretending to be a pompous Senator spouting clichés in every sentence? Or Gertrude Knevels doing a chapter from a new mystery she was writing and hearing a susceptible female guest let out a shriek at a most appropriate moment? Or you, dear Toto, dressed in Renaissance costume, with an accordian strapped over your shoulder, singing and playing an original ballad, and the audience joining in with a Hey-nonny-no' that shook the rafters?

Every month was different, every month had its surprises, and every month we seemed to grow closer to one another. In May we would go to the McF's and pick apples from their made-to-order orchard and then picnic under the trees . . . to part for another season.

We met at one another's homes, but when people began finding it difficult to get to Plainfield—though we told them it was just as far from Orange to Plainfield as it was from Plainfield to Orange—I decided to form a similar group based on people in our area. And that's how Words and Music was born. You and I talked it over for weeks and, since you were busy on a project, I wrote all the letters, outlining the idea and asking if the person would be interested in joining. I got an amazing response, and Words and Music became a reality. Musicians were now part of the membership, whereas with Listen-to-me music was always performed by a guest. The same informality and loose structure was kept—that we insisted upon—and we were off, with a fall gathering here that was the beginning of a group that has held together for ten years now and is still going strong . . . and that got written up as a feature story in the New York Times.

This month, true to tradition, we'll end our year with a fun meeting. Skits, and humorous verses, and black-outs and Victorian ribald songs by our incomparable duo Alicen and Martha. You invariably gave the final whirl a note of your own; there your humor and your inventiveness could have full play, and people adored you for it. Even I never knew what you were going to do—but whatever it was it brought down the house. How all our members loved you! When you could not get to the meetings, there toward the last, you insisted that I go and take a message from you. "Thank them for the beautiful flowers and cards," you said, "and tell them I think of each of them and I'll be there in spirit." And so you were, darling, and so you shall always be. For Words and Music was, and is, half yours, and no one forgets it, I least of all.

This morning when I took Tom-Tom for his walk we met a young girl on a horse. It's unusual enough to see anyone on a horse these days, and I thought Tom-Tom would have hysterics . . . I imagine he had never seen a creature like that at close quarters. It made me think how times have changed—talk about clichés!—since our younger days, for then you went horseback riding as a regular thing and would tell me how you rode cross-country (through this very area) where there were only fields and woods . . . the little pond, of course, is still here, and some of the brooks which have not dried up. You were an excellent horsewoman, as you would have had to be taught as you were by Mr. G. who had been at the Austrian court stables. He made you ride bareback and sternly commanded that there could not be room for a postage stamp between you and your horse. You always rode alone, because you liked to explore, but one day you went with a small group of friends—and of course it was that day that Bellboy decided to run away, frightened by a piece of white paper on the road. He galloped off madly, leaving the others far behind, and eventually, when you lost both stirrups and felt yourself slipping, you threw yourself off.

When the others reached you they thought you were dead, but you sat up and spat out a mouthful of pebbles, which P. thought were teeth! The ambulance came and you were carted off to the hospital to have a head wound stitched up. Mother spent hours, each day thereafter, combing one strand of hair at a time, to get the dust out, for you were pretty well bandaged and for weeks wore a turban effect to hide your hair until it could be washed. I must say P. gave you a lot of attention during that time, and when you went back to the stables you said, "Well, Mr. G., you always said that I would not be a real rider until I'd been thrown," and he threw up his hands and cried, "My God, I didn't mean that way!"

The hole in your forehead left a big scar, and that simply gave you another reason to wear bangs. You see, I do know your thought processes!

Riding was only one sport you enjoyed. The knee that gave you trouble in later life was the result of playing a fast game of basketball with the boys in your teens. And you did well in tennis and on skates, but it was fencing that was your true love. I enjoyed watching you and your Italian master sparring in the big, high-vaulted room, your short skirt flaring, your eyes flashing, your rapier slashing through the air, and then occasionally I'd hear your exultant, "Touché!"

When the hour was over you'd come up to me. "I feel marvelous! Let's have lunch at that Portuguese place and then go shopping and finish up at the Museum before we go home." I was exhausted just from watching you, and I'd groan. "You ought to fence, too," you would say in a sisterly tone. "It makes you feel simply wonderful." And for the rest of the day you would sprint from here to there, full of gusto and spirit, while I tagged behind, hoping you'd give up and take an early train home. And on the train, stowing your shoes and plaestron and head guard on the rack above us, you would sigh. "I can hardly wait till next week. Mr. G. thinks I'm good enough to enter the competition." And sure enough, enter you did and came out third. I was never more proud of my athletic sister, but I never did take up fencing.

There was always that difference between us. I was more than willing to sit and read or knit while others ran themselves ragged on the courts or skated around the pond or galloped off somewhere, while you drew strength from the very atmosphere you breathed when you were engaged in some sport you loved. That's why it was doubly tragic when the time came that you could not participate— yet you were maturely philosophical about it. "At least I had it," you said. Or "At least I did it." But I knew that living on the memory was really not enough for you, my brave one.

Sometimes I wonder whether that's what life is all about—storing up memories so that old age can be less horrifying and more comforting. It seems a strange way to look at it, yet how else can one suffer old age? In your case there was no chance to put it to the test, which makes me glad. You were too vital a person to rely completely on the passive, and though you were restricted in those last few years in what you would have liked to do, physically, your mental life was as active and ongoing as ever.

I think that's what makes the difference between vital and non-vital people—that mental adventuresomeness, that mental youthfulness and zest for living, however incapacitated a person might be otherwise. There are the people full of physical prowess whose mental capacity is near zero, and when they age they fall into a kind of innocuous desuetude (to use a phrase that was popular in our youth). And the others, who have kept their minds active over the years, no matter how decrepit they are in later years, still glow with the fire of youth and are the kind of people who draw others to them because they seem to give off a love of life.

This is the month when we usually came home from some trip abroad. It was good to have been away—storing up memories!—and it was wonderful to come home. Tippy—and in earlier days, Teddy—would run from one end of the house to the other in hysterical joy; the housekeeper would have the house shining and welcoming; the postman would deliver sacks of mail; friends would drop in ostensibly to hear about our stay but really to tell us the neighborhood gossip. And the garden would be bursting with beauty. The houseman-gardener was always hovering around, eager and impatient to have Father come out to see what miracles he had wrought and to hear Father's compliments. We generally had to come, too. Unpacking could wait, and reading piled-up mail could wait, and telephoning friends could wait until we had seen the violets and the anemones and the scilla and the narcissus and daffodils and aconite and primroses. I think Father was particularly glad to be home again because, as he would say, "Now there's still time to get things started in the cold frames."

That's one of my most vivid recollections of life in the Big House—Father lovingly bent over the troughs of earth in the conservatory, plucking the green shoots of various kinds from the soil with a pair of tweezers and setting them delicately in boxes to be transferred to the cold frames on the side of the garage. He always had flowers in bloom before anyone else in the neighborhood— the Hollander rampant! Hoeing, weeding, hilling, were not for him. Let the gardener do that kind of thing. Once he had set out the tiny plants and had them re-transferred to the garden he took no further interest in them except for a daily inspection. But when they were in riotous bloom, he would gather bouquets for the house and inveigle us into the garden to help him by holding the baskets into which he could drop the snipped blooms.

He always referred to his plants by their Latin names, in a most unostentatious and offhand way, but when we would ask, time and again, what they were in English, he would supply the information patiently and then say, with gentle reproach, "It would be so easy for you to learn their proper names, my dears. Then you could converse with anyone the world over about flowers, for they would know what you meant." Futile to tell him that we never expected to discuss cheiranthus cheiri with an Ethiopian or tithonia speciosa with a Turk. He still insisted that it would be worthwhile. I did manage to get a humorous article out of the situation, but most of the names still elude me!

Sometimes, of course, we stayed on later in Europe, and seeing Dutch or English garden in the spring more than made up for missing our own at home. You had only to admire an English-woman's garden—or her dog—to strike up a conversation that often led to a friendship. "How in the world do you manage to have delphinium as tall as your shoulder?" or "What a darling creature—it's a Cairn, isn't it?" was enough to open up the reserved English person. In fact, we never found them standoffish or remote. They were eager to talk if *you* opened the conversation or made the first gambit, and at inns or hotels they leaped up to offer you the seat by the fire or persuaded you to try the teacake if you so much as said a friendly, "Good afternoon." We often commented how unfairly one can judge a whole nation by one or two encounters, and how the English got their reputation for snootiness I cannot understand—they were almost voluble whenever we came into contact with them, and very helpful and interesting.

Those drives through the English countryside— with you driving an American car with left-hand steering— were unforgettable and lovely, and the little adventures we had only spiced the sense of history that seemed to pervade the landscape. The lorry drivers waved us on, the retired colonels from India service told us tales,the litle waitresses punctuated their service with almost continual "thenkyou's", the bobbies held up traffic for us, the gardeners leaned on their hoes and expatiated on flowers, the gentry invited us to their homes for tea and cucumber sandwiches. The lush green and the flowering hedges, the distant views of valleys and hills, the riotous gardens and stately churches . . . how they all melted together into a succession of perfect days—even when it rained! Roast beef and Yorkshire pudding at Simpson's, the theatre, the museums, the cathedral towns, the galleries—we did it all until we were steeped in beauty and tradition.

And we saw the other side, too—the poor teeth, and the terrible red and yellow cakes in windows, and the coal-mining villages and the rows of dreary houses. And highlighting the whole scene the litle incidents that made us chuckle. Like the time we went to lunch with our literary agent and she asked us how we made coffee. She had been to America and loved our coffee but all her attempts with her own percolator and the brand of coffee she had brought back from the States were, according to her, disastrous. When we told her we used a teaspoon of coffee for each cup of water and one for the pot she looked aghast. "Oh, no wonder!" she said, as a great light dawned. "I used one teaspoon for the whole pot!" And there was the lady we met who told us proudly that she, too, had central heating in her house in Yorkshire. "How warm do you keep your home?" Mother asked. "Oh, quite warm, quite warm," she replied. "Fifty-four."

Those are the things we used to write down in our notebooks. Those are the things that it gives one a chuckle to remember.

I must dredge up more of them. If you were here——But you're not here, I remind myself brutally. Can one chuckle by oneself? I suppose in time one learns, but it leaves an odd echo in a room. A chuckle should be shared. Futile to wish, futile to long. . . . At least I shared them with you when they happened. Let me be glad for that.

May

Very dear one,

It's Father's birthday, and I picked a great bunch of lilies-of-the-valley to put under his portrait. They've always managed to bloom in time for this day, even though on occasions there would be only a small handful because of a late spring. I outlined the bouquet with spearlike green leaves and interspersed some big violets for effect. The fragrance, which to me is the most romantic of all the flower kindgom, pervades the room and brings a host of memories.

There was the year we were in Holland on this day and bought the bouquet from a vendor—so big that it took both hands to go around it, all for a dubbeltje! There was the day we were in Ohio and read the dire news of the invasion of Holland. I can still see the stricken look on Father's face, but he said, "Holland may be conquered, but it will be free again. It has always become free again." And so it was.

There was the day we drove up into Pennsylvania for dinner at a farmhouse written up in the New Yorker, and found it closed. But when the owner heard that it was a birthday she bade us sit on the lawn and herself prepared a repast that staggered us for size and goodness.

And then one year we were in Holland again on his special day, and Mr. de Vries gave a party for him. It was the year of the Queen's fortieth anniversary of her reign, and Amsterdam was a fairyland. The people had outlined every house, every window, and the banks of every waterway with lumieres and as darkness fell the spectacle was breath-taking. After a dinner which stretched our capacity to the limit, and an endless succession of wines from his own vineyards in France, and after toasts and songs and gifts, we were driven around the city before we were taken back to our hotel. It was something to remember . . . but what we remembered most fondly was the way Mr. de Vries sat at Father's feet. He had known him for years, visited him in the United States, done business with him and corresponded in between times, and his admiration for Father knew no bounds. With the utmost simplicity he seated Father in a big chair and himself on the floor. "This I have always wanted to do," he said to us. "I revere him. He has been a most beautiful friend and a real inspiration to me."

It was quite touching and, we felt, truly deserved. In a sense it was the way we felt about him, too.

How often you and I would speculate on what would have happened *if*. What if Father had not had insomnia and been ordered to take a sea trip and found himself in the United States and been offered a job almost at once? What if he had never met Mother? What if she hadn't preferred him over all the beaux in her home town—this foreigner, this stranger, this man whom nobody knew anything about? Their love story, to us, was the perfect love story, complete with happy ending, for their marriage was a true marriage in every sense of the word; their trust, their joy in one another, was a kind of leit motif to our own lives. Perhaps, of course, that's why neither of us married . . . we had such a great example before us of what marriage *could* be that we were discouraged from trying to make one like it.

I can still see Father pulling out Mother's chair at dinner and then stooping to kiss the tip of her nose. Or Mother running her hand lovingly over his shining white hair when she passed his chair in the library. And I remember seeing Mother, after he died, reading his love letters over and then slowly tearing each one into tiny shreds, the tears running down her face. They must have been very beautiful, for he had a way with words and the words came from his heart.

Part of our daily living was hearing the loving way he said his pet name for her—Kaatje. And seeing her tie his black tie for a dinner date and plant a kiss on his chin. He sent her flowers every week—and often in between—and for special anniversaries there were special flowers: a bunch of Parma violets because he had sent those on their first date; a huge azalea (which had to be ordered far in advance so that it could be forced) for the day they became engaged, because she had seen it in a florist's window and admired it; masses of yellow roses for their marriage anniversary because there had been yellow roses then. The first flowers that bloomed in the conservatory he tended so religiously were always for her; the first flowers from the garden were made into a nosegay for her. Romance, the deep, quiet kind, permeated our home.

Writing about our parents brings so many things to mind. Scenes from our childhood . . . you dancing to Father's playing after dinner (how you could dance after dinner is something of a mystery to me even now); sitting around a table doing a jigsaw puzzle together . . . starting with one of the United States, and for each completed state we had to know the capital! Watching an electrical storm together, while Father held us close and gave us our first taste of the majesty and awesomeness of the universe. Picking violets in Burnett Woods and while we walked home hearing how a molecule of oxygen took a molecule of hydrogen on either side and became, miraculously, water. Looking into a microscope at the slides we had made of a dandelion puff. Watching crystals form in a jar as the first experiment with our chemistry set.

The scenes are endless, a kaleidoscope of color and excitement and enlightenment and fun. I wonder how many people as old as I can look back on a childhood of growing wonder and enlarged horizon? I say 'as old as I' but you were in all the pictures, in all the adventures and experiments and family adventures. So my speculation is increased to ponder how many people can have had the inestimable joy of sharing things like that with someone as dear and close as you were to me?

Though we were together in so many things, I always liked the way you struck out on your own when something interested you. Ballet, for instance. You decided you would like to try ballet, and off you went to New York, inveigling Mme. de F. to take you on in spite of being older than most of her pupils, and for a year or more you were happy in learning the rudiments of a new art. "I never expect to do more than rise on my toes," you told me whimsically, "if that. But it will be so nice to find out if I can do it." Your ballet shoes are still on a shelf in the closet, mute reminders of your determination and grace. I would never have thought of attempting anything like that, but now, through you, I appreciate ballet all the more for having had a tyro in the family.

You wanted to learn to play the accordion—an instrument, certainly, that had never been in our family!— and went out and bought a 120 bass one, and learned. What fun you had with it, and how many different avenues it opened up, including the surprising one of allowing you to compose such delightful little songs, which you had never been able to do on the piano!

And you decided to take up woodworking. There was an adult education class at the High School that year, and you joined. It meant getting there at seven-thirty and coming home alone . . . but you quite gloried in learning to work with wood and operate a motor-driven saw and to plane a board beautifully, and the boys in the class were quite respectful of you and the two other girls who had had the temerity to join. The scissor tongs you made for Mother is beautiful, and the open shoe stand you did for me is one of my prized possessions still. What did I ever do without it?

If there had been more hours in your busy days I

know you would have tried a dozen other fields, whereas with me it was a case of wishful thinking mostly. I would have liked to do so and so, but never got around to the actual doing or joining. Yet I got a vicarious pleasure—and learned quite a bit in that pleasure—from listening to your experiences. I used to bemoan the fact, occasionally, that I was not of your caliber, but you, bless your heart, were always there with a ready and comforting answer. "You do other things that I wouldn't even attempt," you said firmly. I was wise enough not to ask you to be more specific.

There was another of your essays into other fields that intrigued me. During the war you joined the civilian airplane watchers stationed on the roof of the High School. Bundled to the ears in the wintry weather you never did spot any enemy planes, of course, but among the watchers was a professor of astronomy who brought his telescope along and those who were interested studied the heavens with him.

It was much too cold a proposition for me. I preferred the astronomy nights we had had at home, with the celestial globe Father had bought. With all the lights in the library extinguished and only the skies reflected on the white ceiling it was a joy—in very comfortable circumstances—to hear Father point out the constellations and give us a sense of awe at the immensity and complexity of the universe.

Tippy was always present at these sessions, but after a time he would tire of our concentration on something beside himself, and ostentatiously trip over the extension cord, which then pulled out the plug. Then we would have to turn on the lights and he would look up at us, all innocence. But he would have effectively ended that particular session.

What a personality he had! And how you loved him! I can see you, with him held close to your ear, as you crooned, "You're the most wonderful, darlingest dog in the whole wide world *and* twenty-seven counties *and* outer space." The extravagant words were a little ritual you had, every day, and he came to expect it. I thought of it so poignantly today when I put a little bunch of lilies-of-the-valley on the flat stone that marks his grave in the garden under the dogwood tree. But I changed the words you would have said to suit myself. "You were the most wonderful, darlingest sister in the whole wide world *and* twenty-seven counties *and* outer space."

How can there be anything more than that?

June

My One and Only,

I can scarcely believe that it is a year since you died. In a way it has been the longest year of my life, and the most terrible, and the darkest. But in another way it seems only yesterday that I saw you last . . . with a faint, beautiful smile on your face because you had found peace at last. I stood there beside the hospital bed, looking down at you as if I could never have enough . . . numb with grief as the realization swept over me that I had lost you.

For so many months you had been in pain. The poem you wrote about it tore at my heart, for it came from *your* heart. You had told me time and again that you did not fear death, that when it came you felt you would welcome it. But you had promised to stay with me as long as you could, and you had done it, in spite of your wish to go. Now Death had come as a friend and you were free.

It was I who was bound now. Bound to life, bound to sorrow, forced to go on without you.

I had tried so hard to keep you; I had turned away from the inevitable, as if by ignoring it I could vanquish it. Standing beside you I knew at last what I was faced with, and it seemed more than I could bear.

It was after that that I began writing to you, and those letters have made me see how much I owed you and how I gained from you. They have been my salvation and perhaps now I am strong enough to go on—not without you, as I had thought, but with you. For no one, as that perspicacious editor said, is truly dead who is remembered with love. And I have remembered you with love, with all the love of my heart.

And you are with me. When I sit in the needle-point chair you made, you are there. When I raise my eyes to the walls where your paintings hang, you are there. When I am at the table and gaze at the doilies you embroidered, when I lie in bed under the afghans you crocheted, when I dress for dinner and put on the gold bracelet and the earrings you made for me, you are there. Your books line the shelves, your poems are there to be read over and over, your speaking eyes look out at me from the photograph on my desk.

148

I can never lose you, my gallant one. I have only to remember the laughter we shared, the days we spent together, the inspiration of your struggle against pain, the spirit with which you met life, and I am enriched and enobled. Now I know that I can never lose you because I have remembered you with love, and you will abide with me to the end of my days.

A Note About the Author

Adèle De Leeuw, a native of Ohio and now a resident of Plainfield, New Jersey, is the author of more than seventy books, many poems, and several hundred short stories articles and newspaper columns. Her work has been translated into ten foreign languages, made into books for hospitalized patients, reprinted as paperbacks, reproduced on cassettes and in microfiche, transcribed into Braille, performed on radio, and included in anthologies.

She is a member of The Authors League, Pen and Brush, Words and Music, New Jersey Press Women, Altrusa, and Women's National Book Association. She is on the board of directors of the New Jersey Theatre Forum, (in 1982 she was elected President), Chairperson of the Rutgers University Advisory Council on Children's Literature, and President of the Plainfield Symphony Auxiliary.

Her sister Cateau (for whom this book is written) and she were awarded a joint citation by the Martha Kinney Cooper Ohioana Library Association for the quality of their work over the years. She is a frequent speaker at women's clubs and schools and has often been moderator at Book-and-Author luncheons.